# Praise for
## *Surviving the Unimaginable*

"A wonderful book, a real gem, written with great eloquence and imbued with warmth, wisdom, compassion, and a deep insight and understanding of parental bereavement. This book provides accessible and clear information and guidance to family, friends and healthcare practitioners on how best to provide compassionate care to bereaved parents and their families. Most importantly, it provides a vehicle for the voices of bereaved parents themselves whose experience has so much to offer other bereaved parents and those who provide care for them. For newly bereaved parents, this book will be a "light in the darkness"... words that will provide solace and comfort and a sense of community that may alleviate the exquisite loneliness of grief and give hope that the unimaginable can be survived."

**— Vera Russell, BSW, MPH,**
Bereavement Counsellor, Sydney, Australia

"As a bereaved mother and advocate for pregnancy and infant loss, I am grateful to have found this book. Reading these intimate words allows us to find glimmers of hope and healing, comforting us when we need it the most."

**— Kiley Hanish,**
OTD Founder of Return to Zero: HOPE

"This is a guidebook for the earliest moments of loss through the miraculous minefield of a subsequent pregnancy and everything in between."

**— Shawn,**
mother of Harper and Jack

"We hope that every medical caregiver reads this searingly insightful and compassionate book about what those who suffer from the death of a baby need to hear, how they need to be treated, and how they can be guided helpfully through the grieving process."

— **Dr. Debbie Findling and Abby Michelson Porth,**
co-founders of the Jewish Community Memory Garden
(www.thememorygarden.org)

"Grieving families and friends will find this an invaluable companion as they struggle with what to expect, what to say, even how to be in the face of great loss. Caregivers and healthcare professionals will also find this book a useful tool in better preparing themselves to serve the survivors."

— **Jim Fazackerley, M.P.P.**
EMS Captain (Ret.)

"As a newly bereaved parent and therapist, I found *Surviving the Unimaginable* a deeply touching, validating and practical guide to navigating the loss of a beloved baby. As one parent wrote, 'be brave, vulnerable, gracious and fully present.' This book shows readers how."

— **Erin M.G. Arsala, PhD,**
mother of two angels

"Dr. Vermont assists us in gaining greater understanding of this often taboo subject through a collection of voices from twenty couples as they navigate loss, pain and grief and make their way toward healing. Her presentation of their stories and varied related responses and lessons are intense, moving, and instructive to grieving couples, family and friends, clergy and medical professionals."

— **Samuel J. Salkin,**
Executive Director, Sinai Memorial Chapel Chevra Kadisha

"*Surviving the Unimaginable* is the guide that every newly bereaved parent needs by their side while grieving for the loss of their baby. I often find myself dipping back into the book for advice and support."

— **Anne-Marie and Joe,**
parents of Fionn and Ruairi

"As a medical professional, I found this book gives tremendous insight into the emotions and thoughts that are racing through parents before and after these horrible events, and how the right (and wrong) approaches and statements can have such a profound impact."

— **Peter Emblad, MD,**
emergency physician, San Francisco, CA

"As a mother of a stillborn baby, and also a midwife, *Surviving the Unimaginable* resonated with me. It is carefully written to serve a dual role for parents and also those who are their 'sherpas' on their journey up the mountain of trauma grief and loss after the death of a baby. It also provides practical guidance for those supporting the parents. No-one is forgotten."

— **Dr. Jane Warland, PhD, RM,**
Australia, author of *Different Baby, Different Story*

"Dr. Vermont meets grieving families where they are, takes them by the hand and leads them through the desertscape of unfathomable loss. She has gifted the rest of us with increased understanding, empathy, insight and wisdom."

— **Laurie Barkin, RN, MS.**
Author of *The Comfort Garden: Tales from the Trauma Unit.*

"I wish I had read this book during my training as a pediatrician and strongly recommend it to every pediatrician, obstetrician, family practitioner, midwife and nursery nurse."

— **Sharon Guild, MD, FAAP,**
France

"Dr. Vermont has climbed this mountain of grief over and over with many souls. Much like a sherpa guide, each trip has taught her something unique about this unimaginable journey. Whether you are struggling with your own personal loss or walking alongside someone experiencing deep loss, this book joins you on your journey."

— **Rev. Bob Deel,**
Hospital Chaplain

"Vermont's insights from years of grief counseling create an invaluable resource for anyone close to the death of a child. Reading other couples' intimate stories of navigating this time validated our own experience in a way that we didn't expect, and gave us strength."

— **Alden and Olle,**
parents of Hugo, Stockholm, Sweden

"*Surviving the Unimaginable* provides context and language for medical personnel working directly with sudden baby death, who may not fully understand the weight and gravity their words and actions carry during this fraught time."

— **Suzanne Bernier,**
Licensed Marriage and Family Therapist

"When our son, Gael, was stillborn, my partner and I were shattered. This book provides a window into the unique pains and experiences of mothers, fathers, grandparents, healthcare professionals, and other important people in the delicate ecosystem of infant death."

— **Ryann and Simon,**
parents of Gael

"Dr. Vermont's warm and caring personality seeps into her writing and teaches readers not only practical advice in coping with the loss of a baby, but also the most important lessons: grief is natural, each of us grieves in our own way, and it is possible to continue to live and grow again. An intimate and enlightening book."

— **Gillian Emblad, PA**

"I love the fact that Dr. Vermont addresses the grieving process for fathers, grandparents, and siblings--and not just grieving mothers. This book is an absolute must for healthcare providers to share with the families they care for after the loss of a baby."

— **Salina Patel, RN BSN,**
Pediatric Palliative Care Nurse

"Grief is not taught in the typical "What to Expect" books one might read while pregnant. Thankfully, *Surviving the Unimaginable* compiles a collection of raw and unfiltered emotions felt when experiencing the grief of a baby. Pascale Vermont has assembled an invaluable resource that everyone should read."

— **Cherisse and Kyle Eisenberg**

"Dr. Vermont's book is very practical, easy to understand, touching, and instills a sense of hope. *Surviving the Unimaginable* is a book that should be in everybody's library."

— **Gabriela Peñaloza,**
Mexico City, Mexico

"Reading Dr. Vermont's sensitive and supportive book helped me to alleviate some of the sorrow I myself have carried with me for many years following my own experiences of twice living through the death of my babies."

— **Kathryn Cleberg,**
Registered Nurse and bereaved mother

"This book brings solace to the mothers, fathers, and relatives who are close to those who lose a baby, and offers a bit of peace and hope through the moving stories of parents who suffer such painful experiences. I felt very moved by these stories, and know it will help me become more empathetic and sensitive toward families that suffer any kind of loss."

— **Paola Orozco Gallegos,**
Mexico City, Mexico (translated from Spanish)

"Reading *Surviving the Unimaginable* is a profoundly emotional, educational, and empathetic journey."

— **Daniela Cavalli, PhD,**
Chile (translated from Spanish)

"Pascale shares with us her incomparable experience in using empathy in an effective yet deeply warm-hearted way. This book is highly readable and could be used in a teaching context as well as for the general public."

— **Jan and Bruno,**
Montpellier, France (translated from French)

"This book provides empathy from the perspective of a cohort who completely understands the pain and shock that comes in the early days of loss; every angle of the journey has been captured, from unthinkable loss, to bottomless grief, the unpredictable toll on a marriage, to the flickering light of survival, returning to the world, to the celebration of life lost and new beginnings. In dark times, this book is a rare, yet much-needed empathetic comfort to the grieving."

— **Shanna,**
mother to a Sunshine, Angel, and Rainbow baby

"This book is beautifully written and brings honor to the babies and families represented. Dr. Vermont gives the reader many elements to consider regarding perinatal loss, and even those with experience in this area will learn something new from the stories."

— **Lindsey Wimmer, CPNP, CPLC,**
Executive Director, Star Legacy Foundation

"The stories in this book are stories of "strength, refuge and belonging." They provide couples who have experienced the devastating loss of a baby a way forward to life and love."

— **Deacon Dan Rosen,**
Grief Counselor, No One Dies Alone volunteer.

"Anybody, especially a professional, who supports parents and families through this terrible time, should read this book. It will remind you that you are not alone, and that there are others who have felt parts of what you are feeling. Pascale says in this book, "My hope is for you to find some solace and guidance", and I did. I hope you do too."

— **Briony,**
mother of Bran (stillborn at 30 weeks)

"Pascale has helped us to not only navigate through the loss of our baby, but to also understand that one's journey toward healing is unique and has no expiration date. We will forever cherish your book as we continue to grieve for our son and hopefully welcome his new baby brother/sister to Earthside soon."

— **Tia and Nick Mastora,**
bereaved parents to Dominic

"Pascale came and sat in my living-room after our son was born prematurely and did not survive. If you are in a position to read this book, I am so sorry, but you are in gentle hands that guided us onto a path of healing."

— **Emily, M.,**
mother of Theo

STORIES OF COPING WITH
PREGNANCY & INFANCY LOSS

# Surviving
## The
# Unimaginable

PASCALE VERMONT, PHD

*Surviving the Unimaginable* is published by Kat Biggie Press
http://katbiggiepress.com

Cover design by Michelle Fairbanks, Fresh Design
Interior design by Write|Publish|Sell
Photo credit: Nano Wisser, www.PhotosByNano.com,
        Drago Renteria, www.dragomedia.com

ISBN: 978-1-948604-85-7
Library of Congress Control Number: 2020914079

Photography Credit: Adam Jacobs of Adam Jacobs Photography

Printed in the United States of America.

# DEDICATION

For my grandchildren, Kakane Marguerite and M'Barack René. My love for you is my companion as I support parents who have lost a baby.

To all the babies of the parents whose love and courage shine in the words of this book: Archer, Cole, Dominic, George, Jack, Jonah, Hunter, Isla, John, Juliet, Kian, Lena, Matteo, Nayeli, Neil, Olan, Sam, Spencer, Stanley and Tino.

My deepest gratitude to the parents who made this book possible by sharing their stories and grief journey: Abigail, Alex & Joel, Alice, Alyssa, Amanda & Tim, Amandine & Shahrukh, Christie & Wayne, Christine & André, Debbie, Emily & Gerry, Julia & David, Justyna & Adrien, Katherine, Katy & Lance, Lena & Luis, Mandy & Sean, Michelle & Aaron, Nathalie & Carl, Nidhi & Venkat, Rebecca & Robert, Sara & Jay, and Sophie & Ryan.

For my children, Cécile, Vanessa and Nicky--your love sustains me in all I do.

# THE UNBROKEN

There is brokenness
out of which comes the unbroken,
a shatteredness out
of which blooms the unshatterable.

There is a sorrow
beyond all grief which leads to joy
and a fragility
out of whose depths emerges strength.

There is a hollow space
too vast for words
through which we pass with each loss,
out of whose darkness
we are sanctioned into being.

There is a cry deeper than all sound
whose serrated edges cut the heart
as we break open to the place inside which is unbreakable
and whole,
while learning to sing.

Rashani, 2003

# TABLE OF CONTENTS

# FOREWORD

I WAS TOUCHED AND HONORED to be asked to write the foreword for this relevant, substantive book. Pascale Vermont and I have been colleagues and friends for many years. She is a talented clinician whose work is held in great respect. Her skill in guiding grieving people from a place of despair to one of well-being is now documented in this work, from which both mourning individuals and the professionals supporting them can benefit.

"Grief never ends, but it changes. It is a passage, not a place to stay. Grief is not a sign of weakness not a lack of faith: it is the price of love." Author unknown.

In this lovely, very approachable book, Pascale Vermont shares insight gained through her years of counseling work with bereaved parents. The personal stories, both her own and those from her clients, will be a guiding star to parents trying to navigate the raw grief after experiencing the death of their baby during pregnancy or infancy.

Reading Dr. Vermont's kind, gentle manner of supporting aching hearts is comforting to read and can help the healing process begin. Her capacity for caring assists parents to communicate their needs, and acknowledge their fragility and vulnerability to one another and to the people who love them and want to help. Parents may recognize themselves, and their own challenges, as they learn the ways in which other families have moved from heart-wrenching devastation to recovering a sense of balance and peace.

The poet David Lehman eloquently captures the spectrum of emotions expressed throughout this powerful book. In his poem of December 19, 2002, published in The Art of Losing, he writes:

It seemed nothing would ever be the same;
This feeling lasted for months.

Not a day passed without a dozen mentions

of the devastation and the grief.

Then life came back

it returned like sap to the tree…

Shooting new life into the veins

of parched leaves—turning them green.

With the guidance of Dr. Vermont's wisdom, grieving parents and other family members can share the hope of knowing that, "Then life came back."

This moving and compassionate book is an important contribution to the body of literature addressing loss and the emotional health and well-being of parents who are traversing challenging, uncharted waters. Written with honesty and sensitivity, it is a valuable resource, not only for the text of the book, but also for the wealth of referral sources it contains. Both clinicians and their clients will appreciate the care and love with which this book was crafted.

**Dr. Kathy Nicholson Hull**
Founder, George Mark Children's House

# Preface

*Working with the traumatically bereaved requires a degree of compassion where we go with others in the place where they are weak, vulnerable, lonely and broken. Our greatest gift is our ability to enter into solidarity with those who suffer.*

Henri Nouwen,
*The Way of the Heart, 1981*

## An Important Lesson

MY FIRST TEACHER WHO taught me how to sit with deep pain and discomfort was a dying man. As a novice palliative care counselor I was asked by a nurse to visit Rob, a man dying of pancreatic cancer. I knew nothing else about him, not his age, marital status, previous career, or any of the information we use to interact with strangers. As I walked into Rob's hospital room, I was assaulted by a pervasive odor of decay and I wanted to run. I felt foolish for having previously believed I had an affinity for the dying and possessed what it took to support them in their transition from life.

But I also sensed there was an important lesson for me to learn. Because Rob appeared to be unconscious I had to find another way to reach him. I decided to inhale deeply, to not give into my instinct to shield myself, but instead to offer my breath as a way to connect to him. I remember thinking how courageous Rob was to show me his barest vulnerability and wanting to express my gratitude. I approached the bed, pulled up a chair next to Rob and took his hand. I had been told that hearing is the last sense to disappear before death, and I spoke to him: "My name is Pascale and I thank you for allowing me to sit with you. If it's okay with you I will take your hand and will just sit here quietly with you. I'm going to breathe with you. There is nothing I need you to do for me." As I matched my breathing to Rob's, our only possible language at this time, I found that my own heart began beating more calmly and that I was no longer focusing on the smell. In fact, Rob had become my first guide in tolerating pain and fear.

I have carried the lesson I learned from Rob into my work as a grief counselor. My most important contribution is to be a companion to the pain of others. This is quite challenging as our natural response to difficulty is to attempt to fix pain in others, partly in an effort to minimize our intolerance of it.

Initially, I would desperately search for the perfect words that would soften the pain of the bereaved parents I met. Soon it became very clear that, not only is it futile to try to fix their pain, but the many feelings associated with pain are a necessary part of the grief journey toward healing. With empathy and respect for each couple I have been asked to support, I know my most important mission is to listen deeply and to understand the meaning of their loss so I can guide them toward healing.

## Learning From Experience

There are life lessons one does not want to learn and, for me, it came in the form of losing my twin grandchildren when my daughter went into premature labor at five months of pregnancy. I will never forget the moment of sheer terror when we called the paramedics and I watched her being taken from her house on a stretcher with her husband by her side. My daughter and her husband's trajectory through this loss was very similar to the experiences of the parents I have worked with, both before this family trauma and after. They felt overwhelmed and unprepared for the many decisions they had to make at the hospital. They did not feel supported by the medical staff and, once home, they felt the deepest sorrow for a very long time. My own pain was a massive double loss—the loss of the ability to protect my daughter from such a trauma and the loss of my own grandchildren.

My role with my daughter was that of a loving mother, not a counselor, yet when I was able to return to my work with grieving parents, I was committed to use what I learned. With a deeper understanding of my own pain, and that of my daughter and her husband, I have been able to connect to couples with more compassion. I developed a broader understanding of the many phases of grief and the detours one must take to find some degree of footing toward enjoying life again. I would love nothing more than to have my grandchildren in my life today, but working through my own grief process, I now know to thank them and their parents for guiding my words and behavior in my work.

## My Role As A Grief Counselor To Bereaved Parents

Early in my counseling work with bereaved parents I was very fortunate to meet someone who would become a mentor to me, Vera Russell,[1] at the annual conference of the Association for Death Education and Counseling (ADEC).[2] Vera spoke in moving and compelling fashion about her work providing grief counseling in New South Wales, Australia, to parents whose children had died of cancer. She called her work *Kitchen Table Counseling* because she drove all over the state to meet people in their homes. She shared with me the guiding values, the theoretical underpinnings of her work, and how she sees her role as a grief counselor. Because her thoughts, formed over a thirty-year-period, resonated so well with me, I have incorporated many of them into my work.

### Guiding as a "Sherpa"

What Tedeschi and Calhoun[3] call 'expert companionship,' Vera refers to as being a 'sherpa' to grieving parents. In a recent interview about her role as a grief counselor, Vera said:

> Imagine climbing Everest for the first time, with me who has done it before. People who are climbing Everest have different gear, heights, gender, experience, and energy. The sherpa pitches the advice on the climb according to what they see the person needing or being capable of at a particular time, *It's time to put on your oxygen mask,* or, *have a rest,* or, *hang on, I see a storm coming and we need to seek shelter.* Or I might

say, *Don't look ahead, it's too early* to discourage them from looking at the future.

I find the metaphor of a sherpa helpful, most importantly, when I accompany parents through their grief process and I can reassure them that their feelings are natural under the circumstances, even when the emotions are new to them. In addition, I can do what family and friends often find very difficult to do because of their own grief—tolerate their intense feelings without burning out. By creating an atmosphere of safety and trust, parents learn they can be completely themselves with me. I convey to them that I am here with them for the long haul, that I will listen actively, remain engaged in our discussions and keep holding up hope that they will survive.

The expertise component comes from having accompanied many other grieving parents and from having learned a fair amount from grief theorists about the various aspects of grief and the path toward healing. Therefore, if I think it might be useful, I share with my new couples what other parents have found helpful in order to prepare them for various challenges ahead. I may also teach them some stress-management techniques to reduce anxiety or self-care techniques that others have used successfully.

Through their words I learn what their pregnancy meant to them and what their hopes were about their future lives with their baby. I serve as a mirror and reflect back to them the validity of their feelings and their clear love for their baby. I acknowledge both their individual and relationship strengths as they become apparent over time to serve as tools in reaching a *new normal*.

### Meeting Parents at Home

Following Vera's example in Australia, I visit parents in their homes instead of having them come to my home office. Not only does this help parents who have little energy to drive to an office when they are paralyzed with sorrow, but it also establishes our relationship to be a collaboration. I meet them on their turf and share my knowledge and support with them. I also find that I learn more about them by being in their environment.

### *Bearing Witness to Change & New Meaning*

Although bereaved parents long to return to their previous selves, with time they discover that they are changed by the experience. As a grief counselor, I bear witness to these changes and gently guide parents to adapt to new circumstances and new ways of looking at the world. Vera said, "It is almost like being a midwife or participating in a rebirth—parents are essentially giving birth to new parts of themselves while retaining some parts of their previous selves."[1] As parents decide on new meaning and new priorities in their lives, they often search for ways to integrate their baby's existence and influence into their family narrative.

# The Mission of this Book

However much I learned about pregnancy and infancy loss through countless webinars and books, as well as becoming a Certified Thanatologist through ADEC—bereaved parents, and their babies by extension, have been my main teachers. I have great admiration for these parents' courage and vulnerability.

Most of my referrals for counseling have come from the Integrated Pediatric Pain and Palliative Care Program at the University of California San Francisco Benioff Children's hospital. After a couple loses a baby, a social worker will ask them if they wish for extra support once they leave the hospital. I am given the names of those parents who request grief counseling and see them as long as they wish. I have also supported many parents who get pregnant again after a loss and who are very anxious about the outcome. Several couples have also given my name to friends and acquaintances who have lost a baby.

Few people are aware of the prevalence of pregnancy and infancy loss. The Centers for Disease and Prevention (CDC) labels all pregnancy losses occurring before the 20th week of pregnancy a "miscarriage," whereas any loss after the 20th week is called a "stillbirth."[4] In 2014 the CDC reported that miscarriages account for 15-20% of confirmed pregnancies. After 20 weeks of pregnancy, one pregnancy in 100 ended in stillbirth. The rate of stillbirth varies considerably by race. In 2014, the stillbirth rate for Non-Hispanic white women was

4.89 per 1,000 live births. For Non-Hispanic black women the stillbirth rate was 10.32 per 1,000 live births.[5] Infant mortality rates also varied according to race, with 4 deaths per 1,000 births for Non-Hispanic white women. Non-Hispanic black women had the highest rate of infant mortality with 11.4 deaths per 1,000 births.[6]

After providing grief counseling to about one hundred couples I realized that their stories needed to be told. Pregnancy and infancy loss are topics most people know very little about. Until fairly recently the loss of a baby was almost a taboo subject and a cross a woman had to bear on her own. As a result of ignorance about the deep pain parents experience after losing a baby, many couples have no guidance and feel a great sense of isolation. In addition, few family and friends know how to support these couples.

Even though the parents I supported grieved in their own unique way, I began to recognize patterns in their experience of the loss. There were commonalities in the way they navigated the first weeks and months. It was also often the case that partners exhibited different grieving styles from each other. Patterns arose when parents coped with the decision to get pregnant again or when they dealt with their anxiety during a subsequent pregnancy. There were similarities in the rituals they created to remember their babies after they died and, lastly, in the ways they were changed by the loss over time.

Most of the parents referred to me come from a subsection of the San Francisco Bay Area that tends to be mostly caucasian, educated, and middle class. Many couples wanted their stories to be known in order to educate people about this kind of loss and to break the silence around the topic. I decided to interview twenty couples, one-fifth of the total number I had met with, and ask them to talk about the topics above. These couples had lost a baby anywhere between four months and five years ago. To my great appreciation, every couple I approached accepted to be interviewed, and several mentioned they would be honored to participate. They wanted their voices to be heard and their experience to be acknowledged. Today they are motivated to make recommendations to other couples who have lost a baby and to give them hope that they, too, can survive.

Over the course of five months I spent about ninety minutes interviewing the couples in this book. The transcriptions of the interviews have been arranged so that they are organized by theme, and edited or approved by couples before publication. But every one of the couples' inspiring words is entirely their own.

Most couples chose to use their own first names and their babies' names, and a few selected pseudonyms.

I included a few grief theory concepts that seemed relevant in various sections to provide a framework for the way I approach grief counseling, but this book is neither a research project or a book about theory. Instead, it is a collection of the voices of couples who have, and still are, navigating their way through deep pain and grief. Within their stories, I use my experience to offer my recommendations on many aspects of the loss to future parents who lose a baby.

Since I am neither a native English speaker or a writer, I had some apprehension about writing this book. A friend of mine helped me overcome this barrier and asked, "Do you care enough?" And I replied, "Absolutely." My resounding positive response gave me the courage to share my work in a book with the hope of it being a companion to grieving parents. I care deeply about supporting those who lose a baby and I continue to think of the babies I've grown to know from the hundred couples I have met over the years. I also feel my own grandchildren whispering to me, *Write and give parents like mine a bit of hope.*

Ultimately this book provides a very intimate look at loss and hope. The thread that runs through each couple's voice in these interviews is the eternal love they have for their babies, a love that moves me time and again. My wish is for readers, whether bereaved parents or those impacted by the loss of a baby, as well as other clinicians interested in this work, to find inspiration through the words of these parents and a roadmap to move toward healing.

# ONE

# Stories of Pregnancy and Infancy Loss

*It was the worst moment of our lives. The whole world got very big and scary. It was crippling*

— Alex

*We went from being one day away from meeting him to losing him*

— Michelle

I HAVE FOUND WHILE WORKING with many couples who have experienced pregnancy or infancy loss that they tend to be very precise in telling their story. They are specific with the time of their loss, saying, *We lost our baby at 21 weeks,* or *Our baby was born still at 38 weeks,* or *He lived just a few hours/days/weeks.* And they are specific with the language they prefer to use regarding the type of loss. One mother said, *I hate the word miscarriage. I prefer pregnancy loss*—a sentiment shared by many mothers for whom the term "miscarriage" or "mis-carriage" implies failure to carry, as if they or their body had failed in some important way to yield a successful pregnancy. Most parents I support reserve the term "stillbirth" for a loss around the due date, not in the more general term as the Centers for Disease Control and Prevention does.[4] In this chapter, I have chosen to follow each parent's lead and their language preferences. I will describe mid-pregnancy losses, then stillbirths and finally infancy losses—right after the birth or in the first few weeks of life.

It became apparent in telling each couple's story, and as often happens with a traumatic event, that parents remembered every aspect of the tragic time they lost their baby—from the day of the week they were given the sad news to the names of the nurses and doctors who assisted them. Through the voices of each parent, these stories speak for themselves.

# Mid-Pregnancy Losses

## Fetal Demise

### Amandine & Shahrukh: Tino's story

"We had been trying to get pregnant for four years," Amandine said, "and were so excited when we finally became pregnant. During our second trimester, after a 'not so great' blood test result, we were recommended to do an amniocentesis. I was hesitant at first and mostly anxious about the procedure. During the amniocentesis, we were told that our baby was very small and that there was a problem. That's when the anxiety really kicked in. We had to wait for the amnio results and come back two weeks later for another ultrasound. After reading the ultrasound reports and researching every medical term, I understood it was serious and somehow started to prepare myself. When we went back for our appointment two weeks later, the radiologist told us this was a "fetal demise"— our baby had died. We were in shock after everything we had gone through to get pregnant. We didn't want to believe it and felt impotent.

"We were told he had died on February 14th, and he was delivered two days later. The 14th remains a very hard memory but the 16th, the day we met our baby, is a beautiful one—it was full of love, surrounded by the wonderful caregivers at the hospital. One nurse took Tino's handprints which we later framed. Nobody rushed us and all our choices were respected. A chaplain came to talk with us and helped us greatly in organizing the cremation of our baby. When it came time to let Tino go, we entrusted him to a nurse who had taken care of us since the morning. I cried with the nurse who stayed with me.

"At the funeral home Shahrukh got me a pendant with some of Tino's ashes inside. It helped me to keep him close to my skin in the following months. I also drew his profile and my finger around his tiny finger and framed his handprints (Figure 1.1 and Figure 1.2)."

Figure 1.1

Figure 1.2

### Katy & Lance: Dominic's story

"At the twenty-week ultrasound the technician did the scan and he wasn't moving," Katy said. "She revealed it was a boy. His condition, as we found out later, was a seizure of the joints - arthrogryposis or fetal akinesia. He couldn't move enough to develop his lungs, and he had a lot of extra fluid because he couldn't swallow. The doctor said, *the baby is very sick*. But there is a level of denial and we thought something could be done. We felt the pressure of choosing between medical tests that might be able to tell us more about the problem, at immense cost and risk, but knowing that even if a test told us more about the problem, we still might not be able to help him. One doctor mentioned termination, but we were against that and asked that they put a note about that in the medical record. We named him after Saint Dominic, which is also the name of the church where we met, and chose Felix for his middle name after a priest in our church who had been a very happy man. We told people his name so they could pray for him when we found out he was sick.

"There was an afternoon at work where I had all the signs of preeclampsia. We went to the hospital and they said, 'We could deliver you by C-section tonight, but it does not improve the chances of survival.' It didn't register. What we wanted was a few minutes with him. I don't think I got the message that he was dying. We went home and, all of a sudden a few nights later, I felt really alone. A few days after that we went to the doctor, and were told there was no heartbeat. The doctor was very blunt. For me, he died that night when I was alone. I never felt him kick because he couldn't because of his condition. I was twenty-nine weeks pregnant by then.

"We had a wonderful nurse who was a trauma/bereavement nurse. She talked about Dominic as a person. They put a bereavement sign on the door and put us in a different ward, away from laboring women. I pushed, and it was a beautiful delivery. He had a great nose and a little mouth, he was perfectly formed. They wrapped him up in a cloth and a photographer from Now I Lay Me Down to Sleep came to take pictures of the three of us (Figure 1.3 and Figure 1.4).[7] They took footprints for each of the family members present. We talked to him a lot. We had taken him to the aquarium and other places when I was pregnant with him, and felt we knew our son. We told him about our family, about all the things he would never find out.

"They turned the air conditioning on very cold to preserve him. We had him in a bassinet next to us like all other parents. It felt like the spirit of the baby was all around us. He is the spiritual leader in the family. We had religious icons in the room, so people knew that was important to us. The resident came over to us and said, *God bless you.* That was a real human moment when someone cared.

"The hospital let us have his body with us as long as we needed. The hardest thing was to choose the moment to let him go. We needed to hold onto things of his, like his hair, and the blanket they had wrapped him in, as proof that he had existed."

Figure 1.3

Figure 1.4

### *Pregnancy Termination*

### *Sara & Jay: Lena's story*

"After years of infertility, and finally having one child through In Vitro Fertilization (IVF), we got pregnant again," Sara said. "About a week after the chorionic villus sampling test, I noticed I was losing a bit of fluid. At the twenty-week ultrasound we got into the room with the technician, and she was very quiet. The body language was that something was wrong. She said she was going to get the doctor, which felt like a red flag. A Maternal-Fetal Medicine (MFM) specialist came into the room and said, 'There is no amniotic fluid around the baby.' And I said, 'What does that mean?' She said, 'Without amniotic fluid the baby won't have any lung function.' Even at that point, it was not registering with me. I said, 'What does that mean, an oxygen tank?' She went on to explain that it was not an option, that zero lung function was possible, that there would be problems with the limbs, and that she would be extremely deformed. Once that reality set in, I just lost it, sobbing.

"I don't have much recollection of what I did that evening after crumbling into my mom's arms once we got home. I was in shock. Jay was stoic and engaging in go-mode. Our daughter was eighteen months, and there was stuff to do. The last few days before the D&E (dilation and evacuation) were wrenching. They were the last days with my baby while she was alive. Plus, it was awful to be on the same floor as women in labor, to hear them. And to hear babies cry while my pregnancy was being terminated. I wish hospitals were more sensitive to that."

### Christie & Wayne: Archer's story

"Our pregnancy had been fine," Christie said. "We had just announced the pregnancy to our friends, but at the twenty-week big scan, they told us we should see a specialist. The doctor was very callous and dry. He said, 'I can't believe your doctor didn't tell you anything.' We did an amnio test, and he said, 'Your child has spina bifida, so you need to schedule an abortion.' We were shell-shocked. We sought another opinion and spent a whole day with specialists—neurosurgeons, neonatal nurses. It was awful hearing the heartbeat and learning that, if we went on with the pregnancy, our child would be in huge pain, and would need surgery right after birth, and would spend his first year at the hospital with a parent next to him. I knew I couldn't do that. And we have two older boys, so we couldn't do that. We knew we didn't want this for our child - he wouldn't be able to go to birthday parties, play with kids, lead a normal life.

"Every doctor and nurse was very kind and very good at describing what his life would be like, and what our lives would be like. They suggested we take everybody's life into account because everyone would be affected. And most kids don't make it to adulthood, so we would be worried about losing him all the time. They told us we would have access to support groups if we chose to keep the pregnancy. Before we had the D&E, my dad told me he and my mom had a similar loss, and it was better that we not see the baby. So we didn't."

### Julia & David: Stanley's story

"At the twenty-week scan, after an easy pregnancy, the ultrasound technician saw several abnormalities, and the doctor came in." Julia said, "I was visibly shaking on the table, feeling completely unprepared and thinking, *I don't want an unwell baby.* I had worked with unwell children, and I've seen people go through challenging times managing them, so I knew it was not for me. We had a fetal ECG (electrocardiogram), and the heart was good, so that gave us some hope, but it was followed by an MRI (magnetic resonance imaging), which was horrific. I was shaking."

David added, "It was the worst I'd ever seen Julia, the worst day of our lives. And then we had the amniocentesis, and were told two weeks later that the results were abnormal." Julia said, "The genetic counselor listed mental, intellectual, and social retardation, a big forehead, failure to thrive...She said he had a condition called balanced translocation and was missing part of his corpus callosum, and might not survive until birth or beyond it." Julia continued, "We scheduled a D&E and were put in triage, in Labor and Delivery, with newborn babies—how much more could I take?"

David explained how he felt during the procedure, sitting in the waiting room. "It was the first time I had sat in a waiting room while the person who is the closest to me was undergoing something so major and sitting by myself. That was very difficult. I remember where I sat, what the room looked like, everything. After the termination, they took blood from both of us to check for the genetic condition. They asked if we wanted footprints or photos. I remember thinking it would be quite nice to have a tangible thing from the baby, an acknowledgment that something existed, but Julia 'did not want any more traumatic memories.' We have the ultrasound photos, which I keep in a box."

Julia said, "Within three minutes of coming to, the social worker was there with a pack of information and resources. I'm glad they realized there was a big emotional toll as a result of this, but this was too soon. I was dealing with the physical side of things, and was not thinking about grief yet. I was in shock."

### Justyna & Adrien: Matteo's story

"It was the end of September," Adrien said. "The doctors told us there were problems. The baby had PUV (posterior urethral valve), which would cause the bladder to inflate and make the evacuation of urine difficult. He would have severe kidney problems, which could cause death in-utero, or require a kidney transplant, possibly at birth, and would overall dictate a strongly medicalized life. Plus, Justyna had a condition called placenta accreta, a serious condition where the placenta grows too deeply into the uterine wall, which can cause severe blood loss during delivery, damage to organs and even death. It was a case of life and death for the baby and for the mother."

Justyna said, "We perceived the risks very differently. I was more ready to take risks to become a mother again. I held onto hope as long as I could but finally reached the decision to terminate the pregnancy, which was a very serious surgery since it included a hysterectomy. I was losing my baby and my uterus, so I knew I was saying goodbye to giving our daughter a brother or sister."

Adrien said, "It was very hard to wait alone during the surgery. It was a very intense day. What affected me the most was passing the point of no return—we were facing either heavy surgery for Justyna with very serious risks or a hysterectomy for her in addition to the loss of our baby."

Both Adrien and Justyna wanted to meet their baby. Adrien said, "Since I did not carry the baby, I wanted to meet him and get a bit of closure." Justyna added, "It helped me to hear him say he wanted to see the baby, and that he held Matteo and kept him next to us for several hours. The staff organized to have pictures of him taken, along with handprints and footprints. It was such a thoughtful gesture and it helped us feel like we were taking some of him home with us, like new parents do. We had no clue about what to do and needed some guidance. The staff prepared us a few days ahead for all the decisions to be made instead of being asked in the moment. They were very helpful at educating us so we could make a decision. We also thought about our daughter, and thought she might want to know her little brother when she's bigger. Now I have two scars—one for my daughter, which is a positive one, and another one for Matteo. I tell myself, *this is my story*."

### Nathalie & Carl: Sam's story

"When we went in for the anatomy scan at twenty weeks, we could see on the screen that there were too many toes and fingers. There was an extra digit on both hands and feet," Nathalie said. "My heart started racing and my stomach dropped. They also told us the other issue was a problem with the vermis, the last part of the cerebellum to develop. They told us in a very clinical manner that we needed an MRI and an amnio, not paying attention that this was horrific for us.

"We came home, and I remember sitting on the floor, crying and saying to Carl 'What do we do?' So we stopped working and started doing our own research. Carl, being an engineer, created a giant spreadsheet of all the syndromes related to polydactyly alone, hypoplastic vermis alone, and both together, and came up with three hundred syndromes."

Carl said, "I put the emotions aside for the moment, and we did research all day long. I didn't want to be in a room with doctors hearing the news and not be prepared with a decision. In our heads we came to a handful of syndromes that we could and could not handle as a family. We ended up making the decision that, if the vermis was still hypoplastic, we would terminate."

"We then went to the hospital for the MRI where, again, they treated us very clinically and confirmed they couldn't see the vermis, but that it was too early for that part of the brain and we should come back in two weeks."

Nathalie said, "We had such a battle with ourselves about whether or not to terminate. We didn't have an actual diagnosis, but a few very serious possible syndromes. We didn't think it was fair for our child to experience such a painful life. We also considered how the care he would need would affect his future siblings' lives and our life as a family. Ultimately, we knew that if we could have a healthy child at some point, he or she would have the opportunity to experience a full, happy life instead of the difficult, heartbreaking one we believed Sam would face.

We went for a second opinion at a different hospital in Boston. We spent the whole day there meeting with specialists who were much more thorough and much nicer, and we met with a genetic counselor at the end of the day who told us the vermis was not there, and that they believed our baby had a syndrome called Joubert. I remember leaving, sitting on a bench crying, knowing the decision we were going to make.

Carl told me he wanted to hold Sam since the baby had been inside me and he had not had the experience of being physically close to the baby. I agreed and also felt that delivering the baby was the respectful way to honor Sam and that I wanted a chance to say goodbye. All these decisions were a real process. We went to Cape Cod beforehand to sit by the water. We wanted to take the baby to the beach. It was sunset, and we sat on a blanket and cried, and took lots of photos of me with my bump.

During the delivery my water broke, and it went very fast because Sam weighed one pound. I remember having horrible anxiety about meeting him.

We each took him in turns very carefully for two to three hours - his skin was very papery and he seemed very fragile. I remember holding him and seeing the extra digits, which was kind of crazy, but was also so beautiful. He looked so much like Carl, maybe because he had no baby fat so his features were not like a baby's but more like an adult.

He transitioned very quickly so we needed to start the next step of the process. I felt the full sadness of that moment and couldn't let him go, cradling him on my chest, and not wanting to say goodbye. The genetic counselor, who was also an MFM, came in and sat next to me, and said. 'You made the right decision.'"

## Stillbirth Losses

### *Christine & André: Isla's story*

"At thirty-six weeks of pregnancy I had a feeling something was wrong," Christine said. "We had to call the hospital twice before someone answered, and they told us to go to Labor and Delivery. It felt like something was grave. The whole walk into the hospital I was crying. The technician used a doppler, and we couldn't hear anything. She called the doctor and said, 'Mom is panicking, can you come in?' That felt condescending. The doctor was wonderful. She came in with two other doctors, and told us that the baby had passed. I remember thinking, *What does that mean? It has to be a mistake, make it right.* I asked what to expect, and the doctor explained they would have to induce me to deliver the baby. They left the room, and we just bawled. We got home and called our parents. It felt like I was letting everybody down."

André said, "We looked on the Internet to see what to do. It said to pack a hospital bag, pick a name, an outfit, to take pictures, and to spend time with the baby. The staff did not give us any help beforehand about what to expect."

Christine said, "They put us in a separate wing, away from laboring mothers and babies. Our doulas came - they were the best. You can still have a good birth experience even though it's the worst of times. She came out breech, but they did not figure this out until I was 10 cm dilated. We got to meet our daughter, and it was beautiful. We knew the time with her was going to be too short. I put her on my chest, we both did. One of the residents thanked me, 'Thank you for letting me be a part of it.' That felt respectful. They said they had a refrigerated crib, but they couldn't find it. She stayed there overnight next to us. We held her, introduced our family to her, cleaned her up, dressed her."

André said, "I cut the umbilical cord. It felt very important to act like other fathers. The dad's relationship is so different from the mom's who carries the child. It is more abstract, so cutting the cord was a very concrete action. The partner should be part of every aspect of the birth. When she was born, we thought she looked perfect, healthy, of good size. Her skin was sloughing up a bit. Nobody tells you that. I wish they had told us before labor started, *These are the things that are going to occur, this is how she's likely to look*. I was afraid beforehand of holding a corpse but, in the moment, none of that mattered. She was our daughter, and she looked beautiful to us. The best part was holding her. She had Christine's mouth and lots of black hair like mine. We spoke to her and read her a letter we had written to her the night before. In it we talked about the pregnancy, our interpretation of who she was, our story with her. And we went home without a baby."

Christine said, "We picked up her ashes on her actual due date - that was so hard. Then they told us she had died of Chronic Villitis of Unknown Etiology, an inflammatory disease where cells attack the placenta. So we were grieving both Isla and the possibility of not being able to have children."

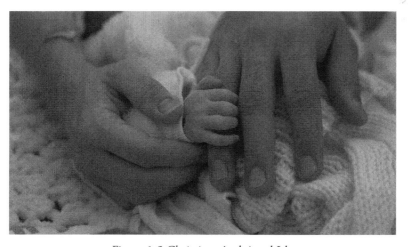

Figure 1.5 Christine, André and Isla

### Michelle & Aaron: Olan's story

"We were thirty-nine weeks pregnant," Michelle said. "Our families were on their way to us. Olan was healthy but breech. They attempted an external cephalic version to turn him, but it did not work so they scheduled a C-section for the next week. We both went on leave from work and returned to the hospital for a pre-op appointment. They went to do an ultrasound, and the technician could not find a heartbeat, and was not saying anything. He was kind of freaking out a little, and left the room. It was so shocking for us. A couple of doctors came back in and did not say anything. It was a slow realization for us - it was so hard to see him so still.

"It very quickly turned to what would come next. We went from thinking we were one day away from meeting him to losing him. We decided to come back to be induced, and to tell our families. That was one of the hardest parts! Somehow Aaron pulled himself together to drive. We had the car seat in the car, the nursery was ready.

"The labor went fine. From my perspective it was beautiful. I remember thinking, *I want to do this five more times, but I don't want my babies to die.* When he was first delivered we did skin to skin. It was very confusing because he was basically healthy. He looked like Aaron, and it was really amazing to see him after all these months. But I felt he was delicate, so it was hard to be at ease with him. The nurse offered to bring a photographer. We were not sure what we wanted but, as we went through it, we turned around, and wanted everything they offered, realizing this was all we could have of him. The nurses were kind, straightforward about everything. When one of them mentioned putting together a memory box, I thought, *I don't want a memory box, whatever this was going to be - I wanted none of it, I wanted my baby.*"

### Nidhi & Venkat: Kian's story

"On the day Kian was scheduled to be induced, at forty-one weeks gestation, I woke up feeling more energetic than usual and all the usual pregnancy pains were gone," Nidhi said. "We did the cold sugary drink test with lemonade to count his kicks but didn't feel any movement. We rushed to Labor and Delivery and, after a series of failed attempts to pick up his heartbeat, the obstetrician was called to do an ultrasound. Before he uttered those fateful words, I could see the black dot on the monitor where the heart should be. The black dot was still instead of beating. I knew our much awaited and longed for baby was gone, just like that, before we could even say hello to him. I don't believe in miracles, but in that moment I wished for one with all my being. Maybe, just maybe when he is out, I would hear him cry and everything would be okay. Venkat started sobbing, but I couldn't cry. I thought I was being strong for us, but I was just numb and in shock. I chose to get induced right away because I didn't want to wait any longer to meet Kian. I was still a mother, I still wanted to see my son, love him and raise him—my hormones didn't know Kian was dead.

"After thirty hours of labor, Kian was born and he was beautiful. Every single inch of him was perfect, but he didn't make any noise. I did skin to skin and Venkat got to cut the cord. No words can explain the joy and the pain that your heart and soul feels when you hold your dead baby in your arms. No words can ever explain the emotions at the loss of your baby and the loss of hopes and dreams of the future with him in it.

"The reality of the situation hit me when we were asked to make a slew of decisions—autopsy vs. no autopsy, cremation vs. burial—that was the first time I cried.

"We spent approximately twelve hours with him. We are forever grateful for the pictures and the memory box they gave us with his prints and a lock of his hair. We told Kian that we love him and will always miss him. Both of his grandmothers were able to meet him. When it was time to send him off, we wished that we had included a toy so he wouldn't be alone in the morgue."

### Alex & Joel: Hunter's story

"I was thirty-seven weeks and four days pregnant," Alex said. "I remember that morning—feeling the overwhelming joy that our lives were going to change at any moment. I was finishing the thank you notes for the baby shower, and couldn't feel her move. I called the advice nurse who recommended we come in. Joel sprinted out of his office and met me in triage. It was very sterile in there, and I started to feel anxious. A nurse put a doppler on me and thought she detected a heartbeat. But it was mine, not the baby's. The nurse ran out and got three more doctors to come in to do an ultrasound. We kept pleading desperately with them, 'Have you found her?' The doctor looked over at me and said, 'She passed.' It was the worst moment of our lives. In that moment I looked over at Joel and couldn't find tears. I was completely numb, in shock. The doctors left us in the room with the lights off, and we felt stuck in there. The whole world got very big and scary. It was crippling. The doctor came back and said, 'We're going to induce you and you will go into labor.' The thought of going through that and not being able to see our daughter open her eyes and take her first cry was debilitating. Hunter is our world, and our world had just crashed. Somehow I had to muster every ounce of strength I possibly could to go into labor."

"I wanted to be strong for her," Joel said. "Alex was incredibly brave. I remember walking down the hallway knowing we were going to the place where we would lose our daughter."

Alex said, "We had a nurse who gave us papers for 'arrangements.' I wanted to scream. The clinical aspect could have been delivered at a different time and in a more sensitive fashion. How can you decide if you want an autopsy for your baby at that moment? How can you think of affecting the integrity of our baby's body before she's delivered? At that moment I was still pregnant and holding onto every ounce of possibility that they were wrong and she would cry. I was so defeated and needed to be treated like a mother and do all the things other parents get to do."

Joel said, "I wish staff were better educated about the timing of decisions to be made. We needed to wait until she was born to make these decisions."

Alex said, "We went through twelve hours of labor and I finally gave birth to her. They told us she had probably been gone for twenty-four hours. We didn't know what she would look like. Would it be traumatic to see her?"

Joel said, "They held her for us. It was a beautiful moment when we met her but it was very brief."

Alex said, "She was so beautiful! They took pictures of her which we cherish and look at often. Leaving the hospital was so hard, knowing she was there and we were leaving her."

# Infancy Losses - From Soon After Birth to a Few Months Later

### *Lena & Luis: Nayeli's story*

Lena said, "Six days after Nayeli was born, the doctors eased us into accepting she could not live. We had tried everything and knew it would require extensive interventions to keep her alive. I whispered into her ear, 'Do whatever you have to do, we love you no matter what.' Somehow I knew she was going to be okay. I got ready that morning, put on makeup. I wanted to look nice for her. Our family and friends came. We had not been able to hold her yet because she was hooked up to machines. We had to wait for the technician to remove the ventilator."

Luis said, "They finally took off the ventilator and handed her to us. She let us all hold her while she was still alive. She just opened her eyes for a brief moment, and it helped us connect with her. We played music, took photos, danced with her, did skin to skin. It was so surreal to finally hold her and know this was it."

Lena said, "I sang 'Into the Mystic' to her by Van Morrison. *Let your soul and spirit fly into the mystic...I wanna rock your gypsy soul.* This was the song that played when we walked down the aisle after we got married. I felt this was the most important thing I had ever done to go and bring our families into this sacred space—this moment between birthing this life and having to let it go, and knowing how sacred life and death are. No matter how long the life, it still mattered. After she passed, I knew we had to go. Her soul had left and I could not stay. We left her there in her plastic bassinet, wrapped in her white blanket looking cozy."

Luis said, "I came back to the room where we had been staying to be alone after everybody left. I had not let myself feel my emotions, and being alone with her gave me that opportunity."

Lena said, "We had her cremated and brought her ashes home. My grandmother passed about eight months after Nayeli. Just before she passed, I was able to talk to her about Nayeli even though she had dementia. At one moment when I was sharing with her, she raised her hand and acted like she was touching a sweet baby—Nayeli—right above my right shoulder. I'm sure it was Nayeli she was seeing. I felt it. My grandmother and Nayeli have the same urn. It wasn't planned—I see it as divine intervention."

Figure 1.6 Lena, Luis and Nayeli

### Sophie & Ryan: Spencer's story

"It was a normal pregnancy until my due date," Sophie said. "At forty weeks I noticed a lack of movement. The advice nurse suggested we come in and be monitored. After some monitoring, they recommended a C-section after the baby's heart rate dropped during a mild contraction."

Ryan said, "While I was waiting outside the operating room, they sounded the alarm in the hospital—a code blue. A nurse came out and said to me, 'Sophie is okay, the baby is in distress, we're doing all we can.' Finally the doctors came out and said they were moving Sophie to a delivery room and told me, 'The baby is not doing well.' I went in and saw that Spencer was on a table with all sorts of tubes in her."

Sophie said, "I remember coming to and the neonatologist telling me, 'Your daughter needed a couple of transfusions.' They said they were taking her to the nursery, which I thought was a good sign, but then said, 'Your baby is not going to make it.' They started wheeling me to the nursery, and I started crying. We went into the room and were surrounded by many specialists. They asked if we wanted to take pictures, and I said, 'No, are you kidding me?' I couldn't fathom trying to capture that moment on camera. I remember asking if she was in pain, and they reassured me she was on morphine and not in pain. We had to decide when to say goodbye. I held her and Ryan was holding her through my arms. She had breathing tubes keeping her alive. They asked us, 'Let us know when you're ready to say goodbye.' We had to decide when to say goodbye to our baby. They were very compassionate."

Ryan said, "I didn't want to lose her, but I didn't want her to suffer. I felt they were keeping her alive for our benefit." Sophie said, "After they cleaned her up and removed the breathing tubes, they brought her back to our room, wrapped in a blanket, looking peaceful. After saying more goodbyes, the nurses took her away. The social worker at the hospital suggested we take pictures of Spencer, but by then they had already transferred her to a different campus. My mom and sister, who came to visit us in the hospital, set out on a mission to find her and capture pictures of her in a onesie outfit. I'm so grateful they did."

Sophie said, "We wanted to donate Spencer's organs to help another child in need, but they didn't check my medical records to see that I was born in the UK. After filling out the paperwork and facing tough, time-sensitive decisions about donating the organs, we were told the donations were not possible.[8] It took eight weeks to get the results of the autopsy, during which time I was wondering if it was my fault. But the cause of death was congenital heart failure—her heart was working overtime."

### Emily & Gerry: Juliet's story

"Our twins, Juliet and Clara, were born at thirty-six weeks of pregnancy through a scheduled C-section," Emily said. "When we were in the hospital Juliet developed a low temperature at one point but it increased again and we were released after three nights. Having had two other children before, we felt comfortable managing at home. On our first morning at home, I nursed Juliet and found one hour later that she had died. The Department of Public Health and the Medical Examiner came and examined our bedroom, making it feel like a crime scene. Immediately after losing Juliet, Clara was taken to the hospital because she had a low temperature. It was a perfect storm—I had just had surgery, we had lost Juliet and now Clara was in the hospital and we had to focus on her."

Gerry said, "During those three days in the hospital with Clara, I remember being very scared about what was going on. I was more focused on worrying about Clara than on mourning Juliet. Everytime a machine bleeped the wrong way, it would jolt me—it was all consuming."

Emily said, "Everything was a distraction from the other thing."

### Katherine & George: Neil's story

"From the second month on, Neil stopped growing," Katherine said. "He didn't want to eat. It was a horrible feeling. Because I had gone back to work, people thought it was because of stress. The pediatrician said it was normal—he did not need to eat more—but it was not true. People thought I was crazy and abnormal. Even my own family did not understand me. The first neurologist did not think it was a huge issue, just a problem with his muscles. We went to Stanford to see another pediatric neurologist. They tried to take some blood but his muscles were so weak that they couldn't get the blood. He suffered for a long time. Because it is a very rare genetic disease, it took a long time to diagnose, basically until a couple of days before he died. We knew beforehand that there was no treatment, but it was not until then that we learned he had Pompe. That was the most horrible time when we learned nothing could save him. I couldn't sleep for 3 days. But my husband, George, was able to remain calm and to look for ways to help. We took Neil to George Mark Children's House, a pediatric palliative care home, and stayed there for about one week before he died. We really appreciated the help they offered our family."[9]

### Amanda & Tim: Jonah's story

"Jonah was born at forty-two weeks after a healthy pregnancy," Amanda said. "During our delivery, Jonah lost significant blood and oxygen to the brain, and was left with brain damage. He was taken to the NICU where we met with various specialists and a neurologist. They did two MRIs. Tragically, they showed that the only part of his brain that was functioning was his brain stem. He started having seizures. After about ten days, we knew he would not have critical functions of life such as eating, seeing, talking, hearing, motor skills. Very quickly we had to figure out how we were going to get end of life care for Jonah. A social worker introduced us to George Mark Children's House.[9]

"Jonah lived for an incredibly special forty days, and twenty-six of those were at George Mark House. I honestly don't know what we would have done without the George Mark House; being there gave us an opportunity to treasure the time that we had with our baby. We lived in a family apartment at George Mark House and were even able to bring our dog, who loved Jonah deeply. Jonah had his own room but rarely spent any time in it. We held him all day long, or the nurses cuddled him.

"What was so miraculous about Jonah was that he was so peaceful and gracious about the whole thing. While we were at George Mark House, there were songs and dancing, provided by a music therapist who played the guitar. We wanted Jonah's story to be about this beautiful - albeit short - life, so everyday we gave him the best possible day we could."

Tim said, "He went into the hydrotherapy pool. It was ninety-eight degrees in there, it was so soothing for him, and he would sometimes fall asleep in our arms. It was such a healing thing, a real family bonding time. There was music in there, and the dog was by the side of the pool."

Amanda said, "We wanted to give him some family experiences, so we took him on two trips, one to Sonoma's wine country and one to the Sonoma coast. The staff asked us, 'What is something you would want to do with Jonah?' We had gone to Sonoma when I was pregnant, and had wanted to return there with our baby. The staff told us to 'be parents and to go!' We took lots of family pictures. I started blogging because we wanted to share his beautiful life with our family and friends. It was our way to help our community understand what Jonah was like—he had such a sweet personality! When we went to the Sonoma coast towards the end of our time with Jonah, we looked at the stars and thought they would always remind us of him, so we named a star after him. We called our time with him *Jonah time*. The greatest lesson he taught us was that you wake up every day, and you live it like there is no tomorrow, and the other stuff falls away. It was a very raw time but so precious.

"We constantly asked the doctor and nurses, 'How is he doing?' not knowing how long he had left. The range was from a matter of days to many months, and that was terrifying. The hardest part was that he got so small. Through it all, Jonah remained calm and loving. His peaceful manner was his way of telling us, *I'm okay*, almost like he had another plan in mind from the plan we had for him.

"We had gone out to dinner with him the night before he passed away because we could tell he had very little time left. We took him to a beautiful restaurant near the water where the waiter told us that our family was a blessing.

We held back tears as we nodded and agreed. That waiter may never know how precious that comment was to our family, but it meant the world.

"After dinner, we came home and cuddled Jonah. At 2am we decided to sleep, but it was hard to give him to the nurses because we never knew if we would see him again. Two of our favorite nurses promised to keep a close watch over him, and we knew he would be safe and comfortable in their arms. We picked him up at 7am like we normally did. I was singing to him a song I love, and that was it - he died in my arms. The last words that Jonah heard were me singing, *I won't give up on us. Even when the skies get rough, I've given you all my love because God knows you're worth it.*"

Figure 1.7 Amanda and Jonah                    Figure 1.8 Jonah

## Commonalities

While each of these stories of loss is entirely unique, with each parent moving from hope to despair as their baby died, running through each narrative is love. It brings to mind Kahlil Gibran's quote: "Work with love, it is to weave the cloth with threads drawn from your heart."[10]

Many parents, regardless of the timing of the loss, not only imagined making a lifetime of memories with their child, but also made memories during the pregnancy. As André said when he and Christine met their baby, Isla, after she was born still, "We talked to her. We told her about the places we went with her during the pregnancy, about the food she liked..."

All parents experienced extreme shock when they were told their baby had already died or would soon die. Their shock was often followed by denial. Some parents held onto hope, even when doctors told them their baby had died. Once they had no choice but to face the tragic reality of the loss, all parents expressed a sense of deep heartbreak, one they could not imagine recovering from. In addition, most parents had to quickly transition from looking forward to meeting their child to making arrangements related to the upcoming loss.

Whether parents need a D&E or will be going through labor—there are still many decisions to make. Will they want pain medicine for the delivery? Will they feel comfortable holding their baby? How do they tell their family? They often feel alone and uncertain in the decisions.

For parents who face whether or not to end a pregnancy because of severe fetal abnormalities, this is a wrenching choice. They may feel at odds with their faith if it prohibits termination. Some of the couples I have supported never shared their decision with their families for fear of disapproval. And many may deal for a long time with feelings of guilt. Others wrestle with themselves when they examine the various factors to take into account - the life their child would have while undergoing multiple surgeries and enduring pain, their potential financial situation if they chose that route, the effect a severely ill child would have on their marriage, and the impact on their existing or future children. I have met with many parents who were grappling with devastating diagnoses, and witnessed them prioritizing their child's quality of life over their own. And I have heard couples tell me the decision to end their pregnancy was "a most selfless act of love" or "the ultimate sacrifice", one guided by not wanting to condemn their child to a life of pain. Lastly, I have heard many mothers, once they and their partners decide on a termination, share the agony of counting down the hours until the day arrives. All mothers, regardless of the nature of the loss, count time differently after the loss, each passing week and month taking them further and further away from the time their baby was alive. In each case, the prevalent sentiment was, as Lena said, "no matter how long the life, it mattered."

# TWO

# For Medical Providers: Support During Loss

*You have a dead child but you still want to be treated and act like a parent.*

— Nidhi

When suffering a traumatic event, a person's ability to cope is greatly impacted by the experiences they have immediately following the incident. People who receive effective support in those critical hours are more likely to recover than to fall into despair. For parents who lose a baby, the medical providers play the vital role of first responder. They must deliver the news of the baby's death and accompany parents through medical procedures, as discussed below.

The couples I have supported over the years have long-lasting memories of how they were treated by medical staff throughout the pregnancy and at delivery. They remembered not only doctors and nurses but also ultrasound technicians and specialists they encountered as they made the difficult decision whether or not to terminate a pregnancy. Parents remembered painful moments of disrespect from medical staff, such as when a doctor announced the news of a child's death in a clinical tone versus an empathetic one. They were deeply touched, however, when a doctor told a mother who had agonized over the decision to end a pregnancy due to severe abnormalities that she did the right thing. As mentioned before, Christine and André were deeply moved when the doctor, delivering their stillborn baby, said to them, *Thank you for letting me be a part of this.* Even small moments—when a nurse shed a tear and showed empathy for their suffering—eased their pain.

I have gathered feedback from the couples I interviewed on specific suggestions to medical providers and compiled them below. Because the preferences vary greatly from couple to couple, I recommend that staff refrain from making any assumptions, and instead, give parents choices. Having choices restores a bit of control at a time of such profound loss. In addition, the more education and preparation they give the parents, the stronger the parents will feel during each step.

# What Parents Appreciated

## Delivering the News

- Parents described being shell-shocked when they were told during the twenty-week scan that their baby had severe abnormalities or that the heartbeat could not be detected. They were thankful for staff who took their time delivering the news and gave them space to process quietly before proceeding to handle logistics.

- Parents were grateful to the specialists who explained how the baby's functioning would be impacted by abnormalities and how their family's life would be affected should they decide to continue the pregnancy. These parents felt respected regardless of their decision.

- Several couples expressed the wish for extra support for fathers waiting for news while their partner was having a complicated and life-threatening delivery. As one mother said, "While focusing on the delivering parent is important medically, it's also important at such a time to provide support to the non-delivering parent. I struggle to this day with the idea that, when I hemorrhaged and was taken to the OR, my husband was left alone with our deceased baby, not knowing whether I would be OK. If someone had been able to stay with him to provide emotional support, that would have made a big difference

## A Space of Their Own

All parents interviewed, whether they were about to undergo a procedure to end the pregnancy or deliver a stillborn, would have liked to be in a waiting room and in an exam room away from laboring women and newborn babies. Those who were taken to a separate wing, and had a special symbol placed on the door to signal a bereavement, were very relieved.

## Avoiding Information Overload

- The question of when to prepare parents for all the decisions to be made after a loss is very challenging. Parents have to decide to see the baby, name the baby, take photos of the baby, decide whether to have an autopsy and also consider cremation or burial.

- Most parents, expecting to carry a baby to term, were completely unprepared and had no idea how to respond. For couples in the hospital, the rapid nature of related questions felt like an assault. They would have preferred the questions regarding baby and parents to be asked in a staggered manner, a couple of hours after the delivery. Those who had to wait a few days before a procedure would have liked to have been better informed.

## Preparing Parents

- Most parents were very apprehensive to see how the baby would look, especially if it had died a little while ago. If medical staff could prepare them gently for what they might see, it would help them greatly in making a decision as to whether or not to meet the baby.

- Some parents, when unprepared and deeply emotional, decided not to have photos taken of the baby, or to hold their baby—only to regret their decision later. They would have greatly appreciated being told they could change their mind in a little while. Some parents advocated for hospital staff to take photos of all babies, regardless of the parents' initial decision, and keep them in their medical record in case parents changed their minds and requested the photos.

## Respecting Preferences

- Most parents really liked medical staff calling their stillborn baby by name.

- Some fathers, wishing to take on the same role as a dad welcoming a live baby, appreciated the opportunity to cut the umbilical cord, whereas others declined.

- Many parents loved skin to skin contact with their baby and were relieved to hear that holding the baby would not cause any harm.

- Couples who chose to have taken photos of the baby and of their family, by Now I Lay Me Down to Sleep volunteer photographers, came to treasure these pictures.

- The parents who chose to spend time with the baby after the delivery were very glad the hospital provided a Cuddle Cot or some cooling mechanism to prolong the experience.

## A mother's voice

After delivering her stillborn baby, Kian, Nidhi took the time to write some detailed feedback to the hospital staff. She had some additional comments to the ones above:

- Reassure the mother the death was not her fault. "The midwife told me there was nothing I could have done. The guilt won't ever completely go away, but having someone with authority tell you that really helps you deal with it."

- Acknowledge the mother's value. "The nurse told me I am a great mother, and I should not let anyone tell me otherwise."

- Give parents a memory box if they wish. Nidhi found it very meaningful for hospital staff to "take footprints and handprints," as well as a "a lock of hair," presented together in a memory box.

- Offer parents the choice to interact with their baby. "Allow the parents to participate in bathing, diapering and clothing the baby. Because death is stigmatized in our society, a lot of parents don't feel right touching, holding or photographing their baby's body. It's important for them to know there is no right or wrong way to express their love—trust your feelings and follow your heart. For example, sing to the baby and tell the baby how they had imagined their future as a family."

- Review lactation options. "Provide the mother with options on how to deal with lactation, such as how to suppress or donate the milk. It can be very healing for the mother—it is a form of organ donation. To know that your child lives on in another infant can be comforting."

- Explain the dying process. "If the baby was delivered alive, and it is known it will not survive, explain the dying process to the parents."

- Respect cultural & religious beliefs. "Be aware of cultural/religious beliefs of the family and take their lead to create memories with their child. And always ask permission before interacting with the baby."

- If at all possible, have someone help with the selection and calls to funeral homes. "That was one of the hardest things to deal with," Nidhi concluded.

## Importance Of Cultural & Religious Sensitivity: A Case in Point

Culture and religion may impact a couple's psychological and behavioral responses to the death of their baby. Decisions must be made about death rituals, including the handling of physical remains, burials/cremations, and also memorials. While there are clear differences between various cultures and religions, there also tend to be great variations within these groups. These cultural and religious differences are often highlighted at the time of death and can pose a challenge to medical providers who attend to patients at a time of heightened emotion. While in an ideal world all medical and mental health providers would practice cultural competence—a recognition of the importance to educate ourselves about various cultural and religious prac-tices—this is not realistic in a multi-cultural society such as ours. Instead, adopting an attitude of cultural humility, which conveys respect and a com-mitment to a lifelong goal of learning from other cultures, is probably a more useful approach.

## Debbie & Abigail's Stories Of Pregnancy Loss

While interviewing Abigail Porth and Debbie Findling, who created The Memory Garden,[11] they shared with me how their pregnancy losses shaped their suggestions as to how medical providers can be more sensitive to the faith practices of Jewish couples and to parents of other religious traditions as well.

*Debbie.* "I was in my early thirties, and had a very uneventful pregnancy. In my third trimester, completely without warning, my water broke. It was too early for that to happen, so I was hooked up to a fetal monitor. I could see my baby in distress, and the doctor told me the baby was not going to be able to survive. I was going to have to go into labor and give birth to a stillborn. It is pretty devastating to know you're going to go through labor to give birth to a stillborn. When I did give birth, the nurse asked my husband and me if we wanted to hold our son. I did and, after saying goodbye, I handed him back to the nurse who recited a prayer to Jesus to protect his soul. Being Jewish that felt very jarring to me...I took him back and recited the Shema, which is the universal prayer for claiming the oneness of God in the Jewish faith...Then I remember the medical provider bringing me a mock birth certificate for my son, like a souvenir, and footprints and handprints of my son and a photograph. Again I was not asked if I wanted these 'trinkets.' I use the word 'trinket' intentionally because it implies something that does not have value.

"While perhaps well-intentioned, these items are all prohibited in the Jewish tradition. There is a teaching in the Jewish tradition that the dead are provided with dignity, so we don't photograph a dead person. We don't take footprints and handprints. In Jewish tradition, life begins at birth, and there has to be a first breath.

"So, now, in the immediate aftermath of experiencing the birth of my first born being a stillbirth, I had to deal with the secondary trauma of what to do with these trinkets. I can't keep them because they are prohibited. I should not have them in the first place. How do I dispose of them?"

*Abigail.* "When I had my miscarriage, I had already been going through a fair amount of fertility and infertility treatments, so this was very much a wanted pregnancy. The process of getting a miscarriage, which went on for several days, was for me a process of watching this baby die. It exacerbated my sense of grief. It was a slow death. After the fourth scan I finally heard there was no heartbeat, and had a scheduled D&C (dilation and curettage).

"When we are feeling grief, depression, and anxiety, just the prospect of seeking out help can be paralyzing. The beauty of being involved in one's faith tradition is that there are rituals for these things. There is a process--one knows what to expect, one's community also knows. In the Jewish tradition, with one call, instantly everything falls into place. The whole network is notified, and things just happen. It was really the wisdom of our sages thousands of years ago to create these processes to handle grief, and it is marked with very specific time periods--seven days, thirty days, and one year. The mourner is to be passive and receive all this from the community. It is incredibly useful for what is the most difficult part of grief and loss--one's emotional stability.

"When you have a loss like this in the Jewish faith, sometimes those prescriptions are prohibited. So I had the contact with my medical first responders, and then went home, and that was it. I had an intense sense of isolation and anxiety. The antidote to isolation and anxiety is community, having one's tradition recognize and acknowledge this was a real loss.

"In addition, for our generation of children and grandchildren of Holocaust survivors, there are certain things we have heard our whole lives about being fruitful and multiplying, and those ideas become embedded in one's psyche. I think they make the loss feel even more searing. I felt that, not only did I fail in maintaining this pregnancy in keeping it alive, but it was a double whammy because of these imperatives I had heard my whole life. This makes the absence of ritual grieving even more painful—it made me feel even more abandoned."

## Recommendations for Rabbis and Other Clergy

*Debbie.* "In so many faiths there are more and more clergy who are women and, even for those who are men, many of them have experienced fertility loss themselves. I would encourage them to talk about it in their faith-based services, in their sermon, in their programming, so that their congregants know they are not alone. We've spoken to many rabbis who said, *I had a stillbirth, too.* Or, *I had a miscarriage, and it never occurred to me to talk about it with my congregants.*

"Clergy draw from their own life experiences to support their communities, but because there is so much stigma still about fertility loss, until people start talking about it, we're not going to break the stigma."

## Recommendations to Medical Providers About Religious Sensitivity

*Debbie.* "After the stillbirth I phoned my OB-GYN to complain about this horrendous experience, which was culturally and religiously insensitive. She invited me to speak at the hospital's grand rounds. I had the intention to scold the medical community about how incredibly insensitive these actions had been. Instead they scolded me! After I presented, they said, *We want to be culturally and religiously sensitive. We want to embrace our patients within their faith, but the other faiths have provided information and brochures to us on how to be culturally and religiously sensitive. They have provided professional development sessions for us, but the Jews haven't. We don't have a Jewish brochure so we can only act based on information provided by the other faiths.* I found this so interesting because, in all the ways we in the Jewish community are so good at educating ourselves and others about our faith, we have kind of dropped the ball in the area of community outreach.

"We expect so much of our medical community. So my expectation of them is not to add to their burden by expecting them to be aware of every faith practice. Even in the Jewish faith there is a wide range of practices. So I don't have any expectation they will be well-versed in my faith or any faith. My expectation of them is to just ask, *Are you a faith-based person? What faith do you practice, and how might we be able to support you in this moment?* If the person says, *I don't know,* then they can call the chaplain. Nurses could say, *I would like to offer a blessing for your stillborn son, would that be okay? I would like to take a photograph, footprints and handprints, and give you a mock birth certificate, would that be all right?* Even in those moments of trauma, we know what we need and want and, if we don't know, we can also say, *I don't know, help me figure it out.*"

*Abigail.* "Before you go into the hospital for any surgery, you're asked about your religion on the admission form. I think the reason is, if you're on your deathbed, they'll know what kind of chaplain to dispatch to you, and what kind of mortuary to contact. So it's understood there is likely to be a religious or spiritual need after a traumatic event or loss. So I think there needs to be a next step. I'm reminded of when you fill out your will, or papers for organ donation, the level of detail is incredible. Perhaps some of that could be adopted by the medical community in a proactive way during the pregnancy. Maybe at the beginning of the third trimester around the time of the hospital visit, not at the time of the impending loss because that would be too anxiety-producing, the OB-GYN could gently say, *Some things don't always go as planned. Let's talk now about how you would feel about that. Do you have a faith tradition? What are your wishes?"*

*                *                *

Debbie and Abigail's experience with medical providers highlights the importance of not making any assumptions about parents' religious and spiritual needs at the time of the loss. They recommend the same practice I have put in place in my grief counseling work. When I meet with people for the first time, I make a point of asking if they have a faith practice and, if so, what the framework is for grieving, for burying or cremating their loved ones, and for holding memorial services within that practice. While it is impossible for medical and mental health providers to be educated in all faith practices related to pregnancy and infancy loss, expressing respect and sensitivity by just asking gently at every step what will bring comfort, is welcomed by parents. Parents may find religious, spiritual or cultural value in the form of mementos like footprints, handprints and photographs, while others may not. It can also be very helpful to ask these parents if they would like a member of their religion's clergy to visit them before they leave the hospital. Lastly, as Debbie acknowledged, community outreach to medical providers by various faith groups would help educate medical staff about how to best support grieving parents and their varied religious and spiritual beliefs.

# THREE

# A Farewell Ceremony
# and Eulogy

*Scattering the ashes felt like I did my job as a mom.*

— Rebecca

When an adult family member dies, there are rituals such as funerals or memorial services which allow family and friends to share special recollections and personality traits of the deceased which will be missed. The immediate family and community derive great comfort from saying goodbye to the deceased through familiar prayers, music, and eulogies. However, when a baby dies, couples are often uncertain about the best way to memorialize their child and feel robbed of the opportunity to share memories of their child's life, especially if the death occurred during pregnancy. Regardless, parents often need to have their baby's existence acknowledged by a supportive community or, if it feels best, privately. I have witnessed parents create customized ceremonies at home when they receive the baby's urn, scatter the ashes on a beach while writing the baby's name in the sand, gather friends and read a letter to their baby about their love and the future they had imagined with them, or hold more traditional religious services. Below are two examples of a farewell ceremony and eulogy.

# Justyna & Adrien: A Farewell Ceremony For Matteo

"It did not take us very long to agree on the place we wanted to spread Matteo's ashes," Justyna said. "It was obvious to us that it should be Hawaii, Kauai more precisely...Over time this place had become very close to our hearts, and was even more so now.

"This was where Adrien proposed to me, where we returned for our honeymoon, and where we rested as a family after the difficult birth of our daughter, Mae (born prematurely at twenty-eight weeks, followed by a long hospital stay for her and for me, after an unexpected delivery abroad).

"As luck would have it, we were able to count on the support of friends of ours there who helped us with this farewell. Once there we first bought a Hawaiian wooden box to transfer Matteo's ashes. In fact, we had already bought a beautiful biodegradable urn in the shape of a turtle, but I listened to my heart and decided to keep it with some ashes inside. Since we plan to go back to Europe to live there one day, I was afraid of being too far away from the spot where we would spread the ashes and not being able to return there. I decided to keep part of them with me, in the turtle, to be able to still keep Matteo close to me.

"We wanted to do something simple for the ceremony, just the three of us. My husband, my daughter and I would take a canoe into the ocean. Making this happen turned out to be a little challenging because of the weather, but ultimately, we were successful. Ironically, during our stay in Hawaii, there happened to be torrential rains, the worst flood in twenty-five years. We had to

Figure 3.1 Adrien, Justyna and Mae          Figure 3.2 hibiscus flowers

wait until almost the last day to be able to do so, and only had a window of two hours before the rain started up again.

"Once the weather cleared up sufficiently, we quickly made our way to a wide deserted beach with shallow access. We climbed into two canoes belonging to our friends, with me holding Matteo's ashes, Mae holding a basket containing beautiful hibiscus flowers, and Adrien with his phone, playing a song we loved. Once far enough from shore, we said a few words of farewell to Matteo, spread the ashes and threw the flowers in the water according to Hawaiian tradition. I felt very calm afterwards, in part because the weather had finally cooperated, and in other part because I was so happy to have been able to say goodbye to him in such an intimate fashion and in this place we hold close to our hearts."

## Amanda & Tim: A Eulogy For Jonah

Dear family and friends,

The sun has set on our time with Jonah. But he will always be a brilliant star that shines brightly in our hearts.

Even before he was born, Jonah was a child of many firsts. He was our first kid, and made us mom and dad for the first time. He was the first grandbaby on both sides, and great-grandbaby to Mimi, Papa and Nonna. As the first of his generation, we were full of anticipation and expectations for our little trailblazer. When planning for Jonah's arrival, we talked about wanting to raise a compassionate, independent young man who set an example for others. We pictured a lifetime of guiding him toward achieving his goals.

When Jonah came into this world, he immediately showed us that he was going to chart his own path. It was a more unique, and frankly much more challenging, one than we could have ever imagined. Yet, he set an example for us and for everyone around him with his peaceful and brave spirit. Jonah gave us the strength to understand that, even though we didn't get as much time together as we wished, we could still live boldly and create wonderful memories together.

In his forty days, Jonah brought us immense joy. He loved singing and dancing to our favorite songs, going on adventures outside, playing on his playmat, and most of all, being held close. Jonah had bright, curious blue eyes that won the attention of anyone who met him. He had long, lean fingers that often reached for—and held your hand. He had large, chunky feet that proved he had his father's genes. And his ginger hair was orange and fiery.

We wish that we had more time with Jonah because he was one incredibly special baby. But the short time that we got to share with him put everything into sharp focus. Following Jonah's lead, we thought carefully about how to spend each day. We thought about what we most wanted him to know and experience. We agreed on several important things:

> *Above all, we wanted Jonah to know that he was deeply loved by us and many others.* We told Jonah that he was perfect and we were radically proud to be his parents. Proud to know him, to love him, and to forever love him. We told him in the songs we sang each morning, and the kisses that Murphy (the family's dog) gave him during family snuggles in bed. Jonah felt the love from his grandparents who didn't hesitate to jump on cross-country flights to celebrate him. They held his hand and pointed out different family traits. They sang Silent Night, wrapped in his favorite blankets, and rocked him.

> *Second, we explained that we were lucky to know a little baby who taught us so much, even without ever saying words.* Jonah reminded us that life, especially new life, is precious and should be treasured. He taught us that we could love more deeply than we ever knew possible. Love him. And love each other. He showed us that joy could exist among sadness. Jonah taught us to be brave, vulnerable, gracious and fully present.

*Lastly, we told Jonah that he would be remembered and missed forever.* He touched the lives of those who had the pleasure of knowing him, as well as so many others who have heard about his journey. Jonah gave us the strength to share his legacy of peace and love, and we are so proud of the indelible impact that our precious boy has left on this earth.

We will forever carry the lessons of *Jonah time.* And we will forever miss our little boy. Our first child. Our trailblazer. We wish that we had more time with his sweet, deserving soul. We are so glad that he has found peace among the heavens. He will live in the stars, in our hearts, and in the new life to come, always.

Figure 3.3 Jonah

Figure 3.4 Tim, Amanda, Jonah and Murphy

# FOUR

# Navigating The First Weeks And Months

*It was a tidal wave of sadness that engulfed us. We did not stray from each other's side for more than thirty minutes for about six weeks.*

— Alex

*We did not want to have his loss define us as broken people for the rest of our lives.*

— Sean

## A Shattered World

WHEN IT COMES TO PLANNING A FAMILY, many couples in first-world countries expect to get pregnant easily, to have uneventful pregnancies, and to give birth to healthy babies. As Alex said, "I knew stillbirths occurred, but I never let myself think that it was going to be for us." Since most miscarriages happen during the first trimester, once that stage of pregnancy is behind them, couples breathe a huge sigh of relief. They announce the pregnancy to their family and friends and start making practical adjustments to their lives as they begin to imagine a future with their child.

However, when a pregnancy loss occurs, the parents' world is turned upside down and they enter a new world where their expectations have been demolished—a concept in the field of grief called "loss of the assumptive world."[12]

This refers to our assumptions that we have a secure place in the world, that we have a sense of control over our lives, and that we have expectations of positive outcomes. Taken together, these assumptions help us navigate our present and plan for our future. When our confidence in the world collapses, there is no longer a safety net or a roadmap, and the usual coping mechanisms seem irrelevant.

After his son was born still just before the due date, Sean said, "There was an immediate recognition that what had happened was so outside the norm of experience. I remember thinking we had no tools, everything was new. It was such a devastating experience... Your life is on this path, and there are so many expectations. You're making changes and preparations for this baby that is truly loved and, all of a sudden, you're on this track that you did not want, and you're doing things that are so outside of the expectations." For Sean, these unexpected circumstances were challenging. He said, "The big picture in your mind is, *I don't want to be here.*"

## A Whirlwind Of Emotions And Reactions

### Trauma

Since most couples who lose a baby often do not know what to expect of themselves or of the grieving process, I spend part of the first meeting teaching them what they are likely to experience. I explain that this is a trauma that may affect them in the following ways:

- **physically:** insomnia, nightmares, headaches, hypervigilance, hypersensitivity to sound, smell, and visual cues.
- **cognitively:** difficulty concentrating and processing information and memory loss.
- **emotionally:** moving very quickly from one emotion to another along with intense feelings of sadness, guilt, shame, anger, hopelessness, yearning, fear of losing other loved ones, and even numbness at times of emotional overload.

- **behaviorally:** fear of being alone at one moment and the inability or lack of interest in being social at the next moment.

- **spiritually:** questioning their faith if they have a religious practice, or wondering about the meaning of life.

I tell couples that they need to heal at each of these levels, and that they may not be able to function as they used to for quite a while. Knowing this helps couples feel relief from their own expectations, as well as their expectations for each other.

## Sadness & Anxiety

The profound emotional chaos of a baby's death often leads to paralyzing sadness and a fear that one may lose her/his sanity. For some women the experience feels out-of-body or surreal. Other mothers experience suicidal thoughts. Often these thoughts tend to reflect more of a longing to be with the baby than an actual desire to die, but they can be terrifying for both parents. Sometimes this suicidal ideation reflects the mother's desire to have never been born so she would not have to live through this pain. Most fathers are more focused on protecting their partners from their grief instead of acknowledging their own sadness.

### Mothers' voices - early grief

*Nathalie.* "I remember lying in bed and just sobbing."

*Sara.* "It was just a raw time. I came home in deep depression for a very long time, unable to take care of my daughter. "

*Katy.* "You feel like you'll never laugh or be normal again. "

*Alex.* "We shut the door to the nursery. Just walking into the house was a huge trigger. We were devastated—those feelings subside but never completely go away. I had huge panic attacks and kept reliving the scene when they rolled her in to meet us. We would be sitting together having the meals our friends brought us, and thinking, *It should have been meals brought to us after Hunter was born.*"

*Rebecca.* "I did not actually feel suicidal, but I did have thoughts about it. I had been prescribed Percocet and remember telling Robert, *I'm not going to do it, but I want you to move the pills somewhere.* I didn't want to have these thoughts; I didn't want that to be John's legacy. I just didn't know how to live without my baby. What felt so real was diving into this grief hole, not knowing how to function. I feel this is an important reality to acknowledge, especially for people who don't know much about it—it is such a taboo subject."

*Amanda.* "My mind operated on two tracks—the Jonah track, and then everything else. I felt I was watching my life as if through a movie. We still got coffee in the morning, walked the dog through the park because we had been doing it a million times, but it felt like an out-of-body experience."

Many women report high levels of anxiety after losing a baby. Having experienced such a devastating loss, they now fear losing other significant persons in their lives, be it their partners, their other children, or even their own parents. They may also worry about their own health being compromised.

### Fathers' voices - early grief

*Wayne.* "I was so focused on taking care of Christie. No matter how hard it was for me, it was a hundred times worse for her—she had carried the baby and had the procedure. So I didn't focus too much on myself, except at night when I let myself be upset."

*David.* "I went straight to great sadness. This was such a rubbish situation, but my overwhelming feeling was *How can I help my wife*? I was putting my sadness in a box and trying to help Julia at a time when things were very raw."

*Robert.* Returning to work, he felt some solace. "It was a very sad, very painful, very uncomfortable time. Rebecca's reaction was much greater than mine, so I was mostly concerned about her. I had just started a new work project and it was very good for me to go to a place where I did not talk about it. When I came home it was very difficult. I did not feel the same way she did. I process things differently."

## Sense of Isolation

As a community we shy away from talking about death and tend to have little knowledge of the impact a baby's death can have on a couple. It was not long ago that women had to bear this loss on their own and, in many cases, pregnancy and infancy loss is still a taboo subject. The lack of acknowledgment is referred to as "disenfranchised loss," a loss whose significance is not recognized by society.[13]

Some elements of bereavement may also be disenfranchised. For example, a grieving mother might be told that the way she is experiencing and coping with grief is inappropriate or unacceptable. This creates a huge sense of isolation. Katherine said, "It was hard because I could not talk about this grief with my husband or my parents. So I felt very alone. All I could do was try to survive."

For many young couples, this is the first time they have experienced death in their lives. In addition, most of them do not know other couples who have lost a baby, and therefore feel very isolated. Lena said, "I had known a couple of women who had lost babies about twenty years ago. However, together we did not know any." Luis added, "We did not know other couples who had gone through that—it was a very lonely experience."

## Difficulty Being Social

Most couples retreat from the world and isolate after losing a baby. Often women fear going outside. Either they worry they will break down unexpectedly or they dread seeing pregnant women and babies. Many simply do not have the energy to engage in social interaction because they are consumed by grief and some even fear their loss is somehow written on their faces and will invite comments from strangers.

*Amandine.* "I could not stand it when people we knew acted as if nothing had happened. I wanted to talk about our son and his birth so much. So I could not see anybody. I would talk to my mom on Skype, and I would just cry, not talk. She listened and helped me to get back into a rhythm. She would say, "Why don't you have some coffee and a shower, and you can call me back when you're done. With her, I could repeat the same things again and again: '*He was so cute. The staff was so great.*'"

*Rebecca.* "I could barely get out of bed. I felt so raw. I had a hard time going outside. People would treat me like I was normal, and I thought, *How can you?* I wanted to just disappear from the public. I didn't want to interact with anyone. I wanted an invisibility cloak around me."

*Sean.* At times he was torn between spending time with his community or needing time away. He said, "I wanted my friends and family around me, but very quickly, I didn't. I oscillated between wanting their support and presence and needing to withdraw. Nobody had gone through our experience, our anger, our sadness and devastation. There are times when you need help and assistance, but you're not in a position to give anything back—return a thoughtful letter, or even read the letter. So I had to give myself permission not to have social graces."

## Loss of Identity

Not only is a couple grieving the loss of their child, but they are also grieving the expectation of a healthy pregnancy and a live baby. In addition, for the duration of the pregnancy, they grew into their identity as mothers and fathers. That transformation cannot be undone—they will always be the parents of this baby. However, to the outside world, they do not appear to be parents and they are often not acknowledged as such. When couples meet other couples who have lost babies, they often provide support for each other, validating each other's identity on special days like Mother's and Father's Day.

A parent may start behaving differently than their usual self. Whereas they may have previously felt strong, capable, gregarious, or resilient, they now perceive themselves as fearful, weak, and asocial. Couples often express to me the fear that they will never return to their previous level of functioning.

## Anger

Parents experience anger in different ways after losing a baby. Parents naturally compare their situation to their friends who may have had easy pregnancies and healthy babies. It may be too painful to spend time with their pregnant friends and those who have children.

*Sophie.* "I couldn't see our friends with their babies. And it seemed so unfair that some of them had had a baby in the NICU because the baby was born early, and they were able to go home with their baby, and all was fine, whereas my baby was full-term and healthy and didn't make it. It seemed so unfair."

This sense of injustice is especially acute for those parents who learned about the pregnancy of a female relative after having lost theirs.

*Justyna.* "My sister was pregnant at the same time, and both babies were due at the same time. That was very hard."

*Nathalie.* "We found out our sister-in-law was pregnant. I couldn't take it—I was hysterical on the couch. It was very hard to be with anyone who was pregnant, or seeing pregnant women. "

*Julia.* "David's sister called us to announce that she was not a carrier of the genetic condition our baby had and that she was pregnant with her first child. I felt she had stolen our baby and our pregnancy."

Other couples who witnessed people around them become pregnant without wanting a child, or saw strangers with poor parenting skills, shared with me that they felt the unjustness of the situation acutely. They knew how very much wanted their baby had been, and what good parents they would have been, and they were angry and frustrated. A lot of parents had a short-fuse out in public, at work, or at home.

*Christie.* "There was plenty of anger in me, and it was hard to trust myself not to be angry at Wayne and the boys. "

*Luis.* "I had moments of being pissed off, and the next moment my brain would revert to, *Nayeli is okay.* Or, if people were cutting me off on the road, I would tell myself, *Let it go, these things don't matter anymore.* "

For some, they felt their faith had been tested, as if God allowed the baby to die in spite of prayers.

*Katherine.* "Somehow even going to church made us sad. During that time I had prayed for Neil so much, and it hurt that the prayers were not answered."

## Guilt & Shame

The death of a baby appears to represent a failure to fulfill this apparently natural role and results in high levels of guilt among many mothers.[15] After a loss, women tend to question every behavior during their pregnancy in an effort to explain what caused it. They spend a lot of time wondering, *What if?* And they don't seem to be able to control this line of questioning.

*Christine.* "I was afraid people would think I had done things wrong during pregnancy—I was afraid of being judged. I felt a lot of shame and guilt."

Other mothers have told me they felt a sense of shame at having deprived their parents and parents-in-law of their grandchild. Nothing their partners said was effective at reducing this feeling.

Some women who had carried a baby with severe genetic abnormalities often expressed shame at *having had a deformed child* and expressed guilt that their body had *failed the baby*. I have often wondered how medical language such as *incompetent cervix* contributes to making mothers feel guilty about not carrying a baby to term.

*Justyna & Adrien.* Knowing her baby had a severe genetic disorder, Justyna still could not stop herself from wondering if she had caused it. She said, "I knew it was not rational to feel guilty about losing the baby, but I couldn't help it." Adrien could not convince her otherwise. He said, "It hurt to see you torment yourself with guilt."

For women who decide to end their pregnancy because of genetic issues, guilt often consumes them, especially if they or their partner comes from a religious background.

*Nathalie.* "Guilt was a big, heavy piece of my experience. It hit me hard after I delivered Sam. I had this thought, *I killed my baby*, that came at me over and over again. When we went to the support group I was afraid to tell our story because I worried others would judge our decision, especially because many did not choose to end their pregnancy.

"Over time, as we told our story and listened to others, I realized that every single mother, no matter the narrative, sat with the same guilt. We all found ways to blame ourselves for what happened. I do believe, as in any loss, there is some comfort in trying to find control over what has happened. While the guilt is extraordinarily painful, I think it is a way we all try to find some sense of control in a situation that is greatly out of our control."

Whether the feeling of guilt or shame originates from mothers thinking their bodies failed them, or from feeling they should have acted differently during their pregnancy, or from believing that they should have noticed warning signs that something was wrong with the baby—I have often thought that it is evidence of the instincts of all mothers, that they are hard-wired to protect their children from harm, and that this protective urge starts in pregnancy, not at birth.

## Grief & the Body

During my time counseling women, many have reported to me how their physical reactions are connected to their grief. A lot of women have opposite reactions. Many women find it emotionally painful to have their milk come in without a baby to nurse, while others find comfort in the "evidence" that their body is functioning as it is meant to. One mother who had lost a baby in her third trimester remembers having the physical need to hold a baby. She told me that she walked around the apartment for many weeks with a rolled towel in her arms. Some women find it ironic and challenging to look at their postpartum bellies because it reminds them of where their baby was growing. Yet others hold onto their baby's "home." For some women, getting their first period after the loss brings relief that their body is healing and is preparing itself for a future pregnancy while, for other women, it represents the difficult passage of time since their baby was alive.

Others talk about missing the labor contractions which were their last physical tie to their baby. In an attempt to remain connected to their baby and remember happier times, some mothers are reluctant to throw away the foods they had craved during their pregnancy or they are unable to unpack the hospital bag they had packed so carefully. Some even keep the milk-stained bra they wore in the days following the delivery as evidence they are mothers. It is as if time is measured differently for these mothers. While they were pregnant, they counted time passing in weeks, with each new one bringing them closer to meeting their baby. Now while grieving, each week that passes takes them further away from the time their baby was alive inside them.

Resuming a sexual relationship after the loss of a baby also presents a challenge. Some women have told me that what they needed in the first few weeks was to be held or touched tenderly, whereas their partners wanted sex as a way to release tension and connect to them. For many women, the thought of intercourse and penetration feels threatening, as so intimately connected to the part of their body that led to the pregnancy. It is also a reminder of labor and how their baby left their body.

Navigating these feelings about becoming sexually active again may take time for women. In addition, strong feelings may come up after intercourse.

Many women start sobbing after lovemaking the first few times, likely from the intensity of the emotions and sensations in that moment and also likely from the hormone oxytocin that is released during orgasm. Some women report feeling tenderness and a bond with their partner, while other women feel so overwhelmed that they worry about sex in the future. By talking openly with one's partner and learning to understand each other's needs—whether they need to move slowly with affection or whether they are ready to have sex—both partners can expect to return, in time, to their previous level of physical intimacy.

## Lactation & Milk Donation

Women start producing milk within days of their baby's death. Some find it emotionally painful to have their milk come in without a baby to nurse, while others find comfort in the evidence that their body is functioning as it is meant to. Many women choose to donate their breast milk to a human milk bank as a way to claim their motherhood, to help another baby and mother, and to experience the legacy of their own baby.[16]

*Christine.* "I thought I could make Isla's life more meaningful by pumping my breast milk to donate."

*Lena.* "I pumped my breast milk for a friend who had had chemo, and had a baby. I would think of the other baby who would get my milk, and then I would go back to crying. I would say to Nayeli in my head, *Thank you for coming to me and for letting me share you with the growth of this other child.* I felt powerful because we were helping other people."

*Amandine.* "When my milk came in, it was a shock. It felt very intense and I had a lot of conflicting emotions. Tino was no longer here, but my body was producing milk that should have nourished him. This milk was also proof that Tino had existed and of my maternity and that my body was functioning normally. I did not want it to stop because it was a link to my baby and it prolonged our life together. I would have given anything to nurse a baby at that time, even if it was not mine. When I went to the Milk Bank, one of the coordinators said to me, *You have no idea how much we need breast milk.* When I brought the milk to the milk bank, it felt very powerful and important, and it gave me so much meaning and some peace. As well as hope."

Not all women will want to donate their milk. However, for those who choose it, it seems to help at many levels. It prolongs the connection to their baby, it fills the physical and emotional need to nurse a baby and it provides a bit of comfort or meaning for the loss. For those women who choose to donate their breast milk, and for the other women who prefer not to, what helps the grieving process is to have choices and regain some control over their bodies and lives.

## Needs of Grandparents & Siblings

### Grandparents

Mothers and fathers spend their parenting years doing their best to protect their children from pain. As their children grow into adults and ultimately live their own lives, parents get used to having less control. Even though they wish they could shield their adult children from the agony of grief they, too, have to cope with their own feelings of deep sorrow and helplessness when their grandchild dies. Over the years I have met with several grandmothers who affirmed what I had experienced myself when my daughter lost twin babies mid-pregnancy. For grandparents, their adult child's pregnancy or infancy loss is very much a double loss. It is the loss of their very much wanted grandchild and the loss of their ability to protect their adult child from deep pain.

Grandparents cannot lean on their adult child for support. Sharing the extent of their pain would just be too overwhelming for their adult child and it would cross some boundaries that need to be maintained for the rest of their adult child's life. Not only do the daughters and sons not have the bandwidth to offer any solace to their own parents, they also need to grieve privately and within their own marriage. This means grandparents have to turn to their own partners, friends and sources of support and grieve in their own way.

Since they need to be helpful to their adult child and search for a way to connect with their grandchild, grandparents may experiment with ways to do both. One grandmother I met with said, "I just needed some validation that I was doing all I could for them without intruding, letting them know I was there to do anything they needed. It was really hard not to try to take on their struggles, and to let them grieve in their own way, at their own pace, just as I was trying to do. I got a tattoo of a duck on my arm, a symbol of my sweet grandbaby, and love it when people ask what it means. I need to tell my friends, and even strangers, about him."

Nancy, a grandmother I met with, had been able to meet her granddaughter, who only lived for ten weeks. She shared what she found difficult and what helped her. "I was so worried about my son—he was completely crushed. It was so hard to go grocery shopping for them and to see babies everywhere and it was hard to hang out with my partner's grandchildren. It all seemed so unfair. I decided to make a photo album with the memories of those weeks she was with us and I also edited all the videos we had of her and gave those to my son and his wife."

Some grandparents have also experienced the loss of their own child, often at a time when pregnancy loss was poorly understood and during a time period when people told them to *be strong*. For these grandparents, witnessing their child's pain can be triggering, but it can also offer an opportunity for healing alongside their adult child's family.

*Katy.* "My parents had had two miscarriages, but had not been encouraged to express their grief. It was hardest for our dads, maybe because our moms were closer to their emotions. We knew we wanted to be open about our feelings, so we encouraged them to communicate and heal from that."

*Christie.* "My mom had gone through the Neptune Society when she lost my sister. So they are the people we called to cremate Archer. We went under the Golden Gate Bridge as a family. My mom, stepdad, and his wife came. They had not had the opportunity to grieve fully, so it was extra emotional to have them do this. My mom said, *I had no idea it was going to be so healing for us to get some closure all these years later.*"

Even though I extended my support to grandfathers as well as to grandmothers, so far the men have not reached out to me, possibly because they are more comfortable coping privately. Here are some thoughts and suggestions compiled from my own experience and that of the grandmothers whom I have talked to.

- The best way to support your adult child in the early days and weeks is through practical help such as grocery shopping, cooking, or taking care of their other children if they have any.

- Some days your child may lean on you for support and on other days they will need to withdraw from you. Follow their lead and try your best not to make any assumptions based on their need to retreat and to respect it. Your needs will fluctuate as well. The best you can do is to listen, show them compassion, and refrain from giving advice.

- You are likely to cry yourself to sleep for quite a while and to experience similar intense emotions to those of your child and their partner. This parallel experience can help you better understand what they are going through. Don't be surprised if those emotions change rapidly and unexpectedly for them and also for you.

- Even though you will sometimes be emotional in front of your child to express your shared sorrow, look for support from other sources—your partner, close friends, or a grief counselor.

- Just as your child will want to talk about their baby, and hear their name spoken, you too will need the same. Give yourself permission to do so.

- Similarly, it can be very helpful to develop your own rituals to grieve your grandchild or create a legacy in their name, such as planting a tree or making baby gowns and hats to gift to a hospital.

- You are likely to notice different grieving styles between your child and their partner because they are grieving according to their individual nature. Respect the privacy of their marriage and let them navigate this difficulty in their own way.

- You and your child will love and grieve your grandchild forever. Don't be surprised if your child's grief continues much longer than you expect—tell yourself their grief is their best expression of their love for their baby. Your child will appreciate your sending them a loving note on the baby's anniversary and on Mother's or Father's day.

- Even though it is terrifying and devastating to watch your child be in such deep pain for so long, have trust that your child and his or her partner will find their way out of their deep suffering, just as you will, and that they may even grow as a result of this experience. Remember that suffering changes us in a way that transcends suffering.

## Siblings

While most of the couples I have met over the years were first-time parents, some of them had other children. These couples were very concerned about what to say to their older children and how to guide them through grief while experiencing their own. Below are some recommendations inspired by The Dougy Center and confirmed by my experience.[17] I am using Emily and Gerry's experience in dealing with their other children as an example.

- Be honest about the baby's death. Say, *The baby's body did not work,* and *He/She died.* Try not to use euphemisms that the child might interpret as the death not being final, or that might be confusing. For example, saying, *We lost the baby,* might imply the baby will return.
    - When one of their twins, Juliet, died soon after returning home from the hospital, Gerry and Emily remembered being terrified of telling their older children about the death. Gerry said, "I was bracing myself for a meltdown and agony. But there was no meltdown." Emily said, "We'd been told to use the word *death,* not *She went to a better place,* and that was the right move. We said, *She died, she won't be here anymore, but we love her and she'll always be your little sister.*"
- Don't be surprised if your child has a reaction separate from yours, or says nothing. Children need time to process in their own way. Tell them they can ask you questions any time.
    - For example, Gerry and Emily's two-year-old daughter grieved in her own way through playing a game or pretending. Emily said, "For a while she carried two dolls and named them Juliet and Clara. It was a bit much for me, but that was what she needed to do. But our son was five at the time and he understood more. At one point he said, referring to Juliet's death, 'I understand it was a very sad thing, the saddest thing that could happen to a person.' He was very matter of fact about it. He doesn't seem to feel very sad about it, but he understands it is."

- Reassure the child the death is not their fault or yours. If your child is concerned that you too will die, tell them you are young and healthy and you will live for a long time. Use language appropriate to your child's developmental age. Children between the age of two and four are very concrete in their language and are very present-oriented; they need short and concrete statements. As children gain more language, between the ages of four to seven, they will be receptive to more verbalization, and will ask more frequent questions.

- Keeping to a predictable routine and demonstrating your love for your child will reassure your child that important facets of their lives have not changed.

- Feel free to express your sadness in front of your child while reassuring them you will recover. You can say, *I'm very sad the baby died*. Honest expressions of grief give children permission to experience their own reactions and present an opportunity to grieve as a family.

- Allow your child to revert to earlier behaviors, such as wanting to sleep in your room.

- Give your child choices in how to grieve. Children have opinions, and feel valued when allowed to choose. For example, you could give your child an item you had selected for the baby, such as a special blanket or teddy bear. And, if you have a photo of the baby in your room, maybe you can ask your child if they would like one in theirs.

- If you have a memorial service for the baby, or any kind of ritual, you can ask the child to participate, maybe by picking some flowers to contribute, or even planting their own small tree in the backyard in honor of their baby sister or brother.

- Children grieve in cycles. They may want to play soon after hearing the news, and then ask repetitive questions later.
  - Gerry said, "Our children mention Juliet's death at the strangest times, out of nowhere. I guess that is how they grieve."

- Let them know it is important to have fun. Taking breaks from grief is part of the healing process.

# What Couples Found Helpful

## Early Days

Parents appreciated the practical and spiritual support of their family and friends.

*Katy.* "What helped the most was the support of our community. So many people turned up at Dominic's funeral. Our housemates were so supportive and organized a meal train."

*Katherine.* "Our church community helped with the whole burial process because we did not know what to do. "

*Aaron.* Writing an email to a larger group of friends and coworkers forced him to start accepting the reality of his and Michelle's loss. "The act of putting the words together was like a bite-size realization. It helped us to have the loss sink in, that this was real. And the messages we received made us feel supported."

*Emily.* "Finding 'information surrogates' was helpful. We had friends who shared the information with different groups of friends or family so we only had to talk to a few people—that was a big relief."

*Mandy.* "The biggest thing I decided in the hospital was that we should do shiva," Mandy said. (A shiva is a formal mourning period of the Jewish faith). "Our loss needed to be held, and the shiva container could hold it. It is a very helpful tradition because people have to meet you where you are, like an immediate crisis intervention. We walked in from the hospital and the food was prepared for the first night of shiva. It set up the context that this was a house of grieving. As a community, it is difficult to relate to this kind of loss, so it gave our family and friends something to do for seven days."

*Sean.* "Through trial and error we decided to have friends go through our phone and look at the messages—it was too overwhelming for us." Mandy asked her assistant at work to send a group email. It read, *At this time, Mandy requests not to email or text her, but to go through me. If you want to be supportive, you can write her a letter.*

## Meeting One's Needs & Self-Care

For many couples, just entering the baby's nursery takes great strength. Often they have to force themselves to interact with the special items in their baby's room.

André and Christine placed all of Isla's mementos into the crib André and his father had built and lit candles every night for months, while other parents left the nursery untouched for a very long time until they had the strength to dismantle it and store the items. One father wrote down all the details of the loss and the labor so he and his wife would never forget those precious moments leading up to meeting their baby. Both parents have to experiment with coping techniques until their needs become clear.

After Emily and Gerry's twin daughter died in their bedroom, Emily knew she had to take a radical approach to the room. She said, "I tore apart our bedroom because she died there. I got rid of the bed, the bedding, the bassinet they were in. I repainted the room. For me it was very important to dynamically change the room so that when Clara came home from the hospital it would feel like a fresh space for her. I wanted Clara to grow up being her own person, not to live in her twin sister's shadow." Gerry said, "We had just experienced death and yet there were more people at home, our two older children and now Clara. We were entering the busiest time of our lives and that was going to be the biggest distraction, whether we wanted it or not."

Other women also turned to books written about pregnancy and infancy loss in an attempt to get both validation of their experience and guidance.

*Amanda.* "We read Amie Lands' book, *Navigating The Unknown*, and it was so helpful. It was really practical and we did a lot of what she recommended."[18]

*Nidhi.* "I went on a quest to look for anything that would help me out. I listened to at least one book a day, and it gave me a feeling of accomplishment. I read books about pregnancy loss and stillbirth. It was very painful but also comforting to know I was not alone in having gone through this. Writing to Kian also helped. I wrote about all the things we could not do with him, that we would never get a chance to do with him. It gave me an outlet to pour my energy into. Sometimes I would write about what we did during the day and how different it would have been with him, and how much I miss him and love him."

*Lena.* Reflecting on the suggestions she would give to grieving parents, she said, "The only way out of this grief is through. Allow yourself to feel the really hard feelings. If you have the physical space to scream and cry, do it. Be gentle with yourselves. Don't expect too much of yourself. Get a tattoo, journal, listen to music, go to the ocean, create a safe space to support each other. It's not going to be easy, but you're going to be okay, even if it does not feel like it for a while. Your baby is living through you."

Many women felt grateful for the support of other mothers who had also lost a baby. They also felt the need to talk about their baby.

*Emily.* "It was nice when people reached out who had had similar stories we had not known about. Meeting other twin moms and seeing how they had come out the other side, that they had a life that looked forward—that gave me hope that I could survive and that the loss doesn't have to be the only thing that defines you."

*Justyna.* "What really helped were the people who were ready to talk about the loss, who used Matteo's name, talked about him, and asked questions."

*Amandine.* "It was so important that he be acknowledged. I needed to talk about him and tell people he had existed and that he taught us so much. It felt really good to show my friends and family my drawing of his profile with my finger around his tiny finger."

Once parents recovered enough to have the energy to exercise, they found it provided both physical and mental relief. Other parents incorporated meditation into their days.

*Rebecca.* Starting each day with a high intensity training class, she said, "I would punch things. I needed to get the anger out—that it had happened to me. Sweating and being able to feel whatever I felt, or cry—that emotional surge just came out. Exercise made me feel lighter energetically and helped me move through the heaviness of grief. I kicked and punched my way out of it."

*David.* "I had a mindful approach—meditation, being present in the moment. I would tell myself, *We've been dealt a very bad deck, but this is where we are today, and tomorrow will be different.*"

*Sean.* Self-care meant cutting out alcohol for a while. "Friends would offer to go out for a beer to relax, but after losing Jack, I knew that I did not want to use alcohol as a crutch and decided not to drink for two or three months. I needed to be present for this to process my grief."

*Venkat.* Organizing a fundraiser in honor of his son brought great meaning. "For me, the first month was about the fundraiser for Save The Children, which provides resources for kids around the world. It was a very nice feeling to know that Kian was able to help other kids."

Mothers sought out many different types of support. To help them through their grief they often incorporated massage and acupuncture into their lives.

One therapeutic approach, Eye Movement Desensitization and Reprocessing (EMDR), was particularly helpful for those with grief reactions that were severely traumatic. Juanita de Sanz, MS, LMFT, an EMDR consultant explains how traumatic memories can be helped with EMDR.[19]

> Neuroscience tells us that traumatic memories are stored and resolved differently than other negative memories or painful experiences. The magnitude of the death of a baby can lead to replaying and reliving the experience over and over again, interrupting the healing process. Sometimes a parent may develop an unhealthy preoccupation with safety and health concerns, or they may perceive that they or their loved ones are in danger, leading to increased anxiety. EMDR blends elements of cognitive therapy, somatic therapy, mindfulness, and left-right brain stimulation to help resolve traumatic experiences relatively quickly.

I have found EMDR to be an excellent adjunct to grief counseling for people, especially mothers, who relive parts of the loss experience over and over in their minds, and who find it very challenging to resume their lives. I have often referred these women to an EMDR practitioner with great results.

## Couples - Supporting Each Other

The couples I interviewed experimented with ways to help each other. Many learned to take some space from each other by going on long walks alone, while other couples did everything together. When one parent seemed paralyzed by grief, the other parent would suggest they return to activities they used to enjoy.

*André.* "Christine would tell me, *Go play hockey, that would be good for you.* Or, I would tell her, *Maybe cooking tonight would be helpful.*"

*Shahrukh.* "I encouraged Amandine to do small, positive things for herself, like gardening."

*Amandine.* "It felt good to focus on living things. Since I'm a biologist, growing plants felt good."

*Amanda.* "I didn't want to be in our home and have the constant reminder of how it was supposed to be with Jonah. So we rented an apartment and

Tim undertook a kitchen remodel. I needed emotional space and he needed to knock down a wall."

Many parents went away on short vacations, or took road trips, or made time to take walks and get out into nature. Some also found being near water and taking walks on the beach helpful.

*Sean.* "This house had so much expectation in it with the nursery. We wanted to go somewhere together to give ourselves some new energy. It was not an escape—we still talked about the loss, but the new energy helped us reflect with a slightly new perspective. We went to the place where we first met and where we vacationed as children. It made us feel the world was not completely screwed up. And we would gather rocks there to bring back to the cemetery for Jack. It was our way of caring for our child and connecting to him."

## Learning From Baby's Perspective

Some parents intentionally used their baby as a guide for them in this new chapter of their lives. Sean said, "When we were having a tough time, we would try to see the situation through Jack's lens: *Jack would want us to.* Or, *We're doing this so Jack would be proud of us.* Or, *We want to give Jack a sibling.* We were finding a language and narrative that included Jack instead of moving on. I kept thinking that he would not want his parents to be broken and he would want us to be in a loving relationship and help people. We did not want to have his loss define us as broken people for the rest of our lives because it is not what this boy would have wanted."

## Returning to Work

After spending the first few weeks together following the loss of their baby, most couples dread being separated from each other once they must return to work. In the first couple of weeks, parents lean on each other by checking in several times a day. I often remind couples that they are still healing from the loss and that they may have difficulty focusing initially. Allowing them to lower their expectations of themselves can bring relief. When possible, returning to work on a part-time basis can ease this transition. For many women, the office is full of triggers, such as other pregnant women or discussions about baby showers.

For men, often they are unsure whether they want their colleagues to bring up the loss. Many men feel relieved to return to a routine they knew well.

In counseling I discuss with parents how to cope with being back in the workplace and how to minimize the apprehension. Most people find it helpful to either send a group email to their coworkers or to have it sent by their supervisor. In the email they may give a brief description of the circumstances of the loss and also indicate whether or not they wish to be asked any questions or even be offered condolences.

Even when parents have notified their coworkers, at times there are people who have not been included in the group email who will ask, *How is the baby?* Most couples dread this moment which Amanda called the *caught in the hallway moment*. Having something prepared to say for such a moment can also be very useful.

*Michelle.* "Seeing people for the first time, even if they knew, was very charged emotionally. You never know what situation is going to be okay. It is like sticking your toes in the water for the first time. Once I got past the initial interaction, it got a little easier."

I often encourage women to give themselves permission to exit the office to go for a walk, or to retreat to the restroom when they become emotional.

*Rebecca.* "I felt naked and vulnerable. The first couple of weeks, I avoided people. I couldn't run away fast enough if people told me they were sorry."

Lining up a couple of coworkers for support while working can provide a bit of a safety net.

*Sophie.* "I had a couple of people I could ask for help. I would be crying in the stairwell and text one of them to bring me tissues. "

*Ryan.* "If people did not mention the loss, it felt insulting. It was confusing because, if they did acknowledge it, that was also hard. And there were times when I wanted to talk about it and they were not ready."

*Tim.* "It felt good to go back and yell at somebody and boss people around. And to do something concrete."

For some parents, returning to work significantly increased their anxiety. They reported they lacked patience with their coworkers. Their anger over the loss of the baby tended to spill over in ways they could not control. I helped these parents find productive outlets for their anger. For other parents, their work had lost meaning and they started questioning whether they should change careers.

They either worked through any anxiety at work or they looked at the situation as an opportunity to assess priorities and make significant changes.

## Support Groups

Attending support groups such as The Compassionate Friends[20] and Helping After Neonatal Death (HAND)[21] can assist bereaved parents. These groups inform parents of important parts of the grieving process. One goal is to help parents create a new relationship with their deceased baby, transforming that relationship from a physical bond established during pregnancy and/or infancy to an internal relationship to nurture going forward.[22]

Through sharing stories about the baby with people who did not know the child but have experienced a similar loss, parents slowly develop a new relationship with their baby. Through the support groups, parents receive much needed validation from other grieving couples. Additionally, newly bereaved parents find hope and guidance by witnessing the strength of group facilitators who have suffered pregnancy and infancy loss as well. For many, they are relieved to be in a place where no acting is required and where they are not expected to find "closure," which would be like losing a sacred bond with their baby.

Nidhi said, "When we went to HAND, we got confirmation that it is common for moms and dads to grieve differently, and that it was okay. By talking about Kian and telling the story over and over again, it helped our mind accept the reality of losing him. Also, some couples had also had stillbirths, like us, and some of them became friends. We would meet and talk about our babies. It was a safe place where we could talk about anything—nothing was illogical to them. People in that community get it."

# FIVE

# Grief Counseling - Early Days

*Give sorrow words;*
*The grief that does not speak*
*Whispers the O'er-fraught heart,*
*And bids it break.*

Shakespeare, *Macbeth*: Act 4, Scene 3

WHEN I MEET COUPLES FOR THE first time after the loss of a baby, they tend to be in a state of deep shock and despair. Often they ruminate on the moment they found out their baby had died or was not viable, and they need to tell me the story of this event multiple times before they are able to come to terms with this new harsh reality.

By showing parents empathy and compassion, they trust that I can hear the very worst of the events that led to the baby's death and that I can tolerate their deep suffering. Couples learn they are in a place of safety and respect where I will not flee from their pain or find a quick cure for it. This, in turn, helps create a collaborative relationship where I encourage them to express any feelings and reactions they may have while gently guiding them to take one step after the other towards healing.

In the beginning I stress the importance of basic self-care, such as healthy eating, moderate exercise and sleep. In addition, I encourage them to cocoon with each other, to keep their world very small, and to focus on grieving the loss of their baby. I also warn them that they may notice differences in their grieving styles and encourage them to respect these variations. I validate how their grief is related not to the length of a baby's life, but instead to their attachment to their child and their hope of a future together.

As I listen to the way parents tell the story of the loss and observe how they connect with each other, I start assessing their strengths as a couple and as individuals. Later in the process, I draw upon these competencies to help them cope with each phase of the grief process.

People in great pain, confronted by a loss they had never imagined, are hungry for guidance and advice. I share with the couples I meet how other couples have negotiated various aspects of the loss, but I stress the importance of following their own needs and of making small choices every day in order to exert a bit of control over their current situation.

As I alternate between normalizing these couples' feelings as being *natural under the circumstances* and educating them about what has helped other couples, I teach them what current grief theorists recommend. In the past, experts in the field of grief suggested the bereaved follow a series of stages toward acceptance of the loss. Now, however, the thinking has changed and it acknowledges that grief is not linear. It is more adaptive for the parents to allow the waves of intense emotions to wash over them and to feel the extent of their grief, and then to consciously re-engage with the practicalities of life—a theory called the Dual Process Model.[23] I explain to the couples I meet that it is a bit like shifting their weight from one foot to the other as they grieve. For example, parents might be overwhelmed with sadness all of a sudden with a need to let their tears flow and later they may feel up to cooking a meal, taking a shower, or watching a movie.

## Natural Reactions to Grief

Many of the couples I support feel great relief when I reassure them that their feelings and reactions are natural and shared by all couples who lose a baby. Because these intense emotions are new to them, parents are relieved to hear they are to be expected.

*Christine.* "You normalized a lot of our emotions and said, *Of course you feel this way; you just lost your precious child.* I would have felt so much worse if I had not had that validation."

*Michelle.* "It helped normalize what we were feeling and made it easier to go back into the world, but to go out there as grieving parents on a very long journey."

*Luis.* "It felt good to hear you say it was normal; that I was not going crazy. We learned there is no right or wrong way to grieve, and counseling played a big role in pushing through it."

*Julia.* "The experience was alien, and it was hard to feel like my normal self. It was reassuring to speak to someone who had seen many couples and could tell us that what I was feeling was normal."

## Two Mantras: Be Gentle With Yourself & Keep Your World Small

In keeping with the need to heal on so many levels after a loss, I give couples permission to be gentle with themselves and to lower their expectations of what they can accomplish.

Christine explained why this was helpful. "My memory was not so good at work. Before I would have been hard on myself. But you told us to be kind and gentle to ourselves, so I said, *You're in a grieving state, and it's normal.* You would also say, *Keep your world small.* That gave us permission not to be social or appear normal to our community. So we protected ourselves and chose not to go to a baby shower or to go to places that would make us feel overwhelmed."

## Creating a Place to Talk

For the parents I meet with, counseling creates a structure and a safe place to discuss their grief and their needs as they evolve over the first few weeks and months.

*Katy.* "It was really helpful meeting all three of us and hearing each other respond to your questions."

*Michelle.* "You asked questions at different stages that helped us see what was taking focus at that time, or what we were not thinking about. And it helped us prepare for things to come."

*Rebecca.* "It was an outlet for me, someone I could talk to who understood what I was saying and said it back to me in a more concise way."

*Christine.* "You did not find solutions for us, but checked in where we were."

*Luis.* Not realizing how helpful talking would be, he said, "I was surprised I was able to open up after telling myself I did not need counseling. You never told us how to feel, we just had an opportunity to talk, and at the end of it, it was always a load off my shoulders." His wife, Lena, said, "It felt good that he was talking. You would pull it out of us. You created a space to talk with each other."

## Meeting People at home

When I started grief counseling to support couples who had had a pregnancy or infancy loss, I felt they would be better served by meeting in their home. I thought it would remove the obstacle of finding the energy to get dressed for an office visit or to drive to an appointment. Instead I wanted to meet couples in their own space, on their turf, where they would be comfortable to be themselves. Not only did a home visit make it easier for them, but it also symbolized that I would meet them where they were in every respect.

*Lena.* "The fact that you came to us instead of having to physically get out and drive was huge. It was so helpful to talk about it on my own couch, and to have you help us on a mental level. "

*Christine.* "Meeting us in our home made a big difference. The logistics of finding someone that fit, and going to them, would have taken energy we did not have."

*Rebecca.* "You came to me. There was no way I could go to an office. It made it soft. There was an ease around seeing you—it was completely fluid."

\*          \*          \*

Grief counseling following a pregnancy or infancy loss serves many purposes. It creates a safe place where parents can start processing the reality of the loss and where their intense feelings are validated. Normalizing these feelings, and learning they are common to all couples who lose a baby, brings great relief. As couples are guided to recognize their own needs, they come to trust that they can cope in the moment by honoring their feelings. As they do, their bond with their baby gets rekindled, and the loss becomes part of their story, one to claim and cherish, not an event to try to put in the past. By learning to alternate between feeling their sadness and re-entering their lives, parents move towards letting the sad and happy moments coexist as they forge ahead. Their heartache will never disappear but joy will eventually be mixed in.

# Six

# Recommendations to Family and Friends & How to Deal With Strangers

*We set an expectation with our community that we want them to know about our baby, to talk about him. It's on us to help people figure out how to do that.*

– Amanda

PEOPLE WHO ARE IN SHOCK NEED to tell the story of the loss in great detail, repetitively. For those who have been traumatized, they learn to accept the reality of the loss by communicating the emotional toll of the loss to the listener, be it family or friends.

Family and friends send them emails and texts, suggest books that might be helpful, and offer all sorts of advice. Although well intended, these efforts may or may not be helpful. With the passage of time between counseling and the interviews, parents were able to reflect. They shared with me the suggestions they would make to family and friends of grieving parents, and the comments and behaviors they did not find so helpful.

## What Can Be Helpful

Once parents start emerging from the blurriness and shock of the initial weeks and become more clear about what feels supportive from family and friends, they can often be very articulate about what they do need from their community. The suggestions made by the couples I interviewed were fairly unanimous. Mostly, they needed people to listen and keep checking in with them, even when they were unable to respond—sometimes for months or even years.

## Listening & Checking In: From Months to Years

*Sophie.* "Be there, be supportive, listen, and be a sounding board. The best things to say are: *I'm sorry. I can't imagine what you're going through. I don't know what to say but I'm here for you.*"

*Alex.* When I spoke to her, Alex remembered specific words and actions she found both moving and very helpful. She said, "Simply offering condolences is a key thing to do at first. *Can we see you? Is it okay if I reach out to you next week?* Making a small effort goes so far. One of our friends did something wonderful. He went and educated himself about our particular kind of loss. It showed he really cared, and it felt wonderful."

*Sean.* "Check in with the person as the weeks and months go by and say, *How are you doing today?* Not, *How is it going?* Maybe they're ready to talk to you about certain things today that they weren't ready to talk about yesterday or a couple of days after."

*Christine.* "People asked what they could do for us. We couldn't respond to emails, let alone tell them what to do. The people who did not ask but brought food or sent a text, without expecting a response, that was what we needed. We did not have the energy for about ten months to guide people to support us. People who came over and did not try to fix things, but were just present and held my hand a little tighter, a little longer, and said, *I'm sorry you're in so much pain*—that felt good.

"And please keep checking in—three, six, eight months later. Keep making a phone call. That is so much better compared to people who think you're okay. People around us moved on but we needed to have them know it would be painful for a very long time and to keep asking. A friend would send us a letter around the birthday, or a drawing, or tell a story to Isla like, *When your mom was four months pregnant we went to a concert and she was so happy and danced.* It was so thoughtful and it blew me away."

*Nidhi & Venkat.* They remembered several friends who acted in very supportive ways. Nidhi said, "The best thing to do is just to show up and be there for them. Say, *I'm just going to drop by and leave something and you don't have to talk if you don't want to.* Some friends dropped food at our doorstep for a week. A friend gave me a knitting project. She chose Kian's birth month color, turquoise. I knitted for one whole day and finished the scarf in twenty-four hours." Venkat added, "Another friend gave us a Buddhist God, a Jizo statue, and included a story about Jizo who is the protector of children. In that culture, parents write letters to Jizo. He is the messenger who takes messages to the babies in the underworld. It was very nice to know we were cared for."

*Emily & Gerry.* Friends and family organized a meal train for Emily and Gerry's family. They were very appreciative of having dinners delivered to them for three months. Emily remembered a friend who was especially thoughtful. She said, "One friend did the best thing. She had kids the same age as our kids, and she ordered food that she knew our kids would like. It was unassuming and so helpful." Gerry added, "I was very grateful for my coworkers who said they would cover for me at work and to take as much time as I needed. And it was very nice when friends asked me to go play golf to take my mind off things."

As I learned over the years, this type of loss far exceeds what friends and family may realize. It could well be that a mother, sharing a meal with a friend whose children would be the same age as her child, had he lived, feels triggered by talk of a child entering high school, going to the prom, applying to college—all family milestones. By that time many people have stopped mentioning the stillborn baby, assuming that *she's over it* or *It's best not to remind the mother of her baby who did not take its first breath.* Even if the pain has now become more bearable for her, it would be wise to continue being sensitive to this mother and to understand she will always miss her baby and hurt when she hears about other children's successes and transitions from one phase of childhood to another.

## With Time, Revert to Normal Conversation

Christine made an interesting point which was echoed by other couples. "After a while we did not want our friends to tiptoe around us. When people had wonderful things happening in their lives, they were reluctant to share. Or, if bad things happened, they didn't want to tell us because it didn't compare. But that can become isolating when your friends' lives become opaque. So we told our friends, *Please ask us about Isla. Please tell us about your lives. We may not be able to show up, but eventually we will.* That was very helpful to our friends and they responded."

## Using the Baby's Name & Asking to See Photos if Appropriate

Many of the couples I meet with are touched when I ask if they would like to show me a photo of their baby. Before asking, I use my intuition and listen to and observe a couple's verbal and non-verbal communication when they speak about the moment they met their baby. This often feels quite risky, as the photos are so very intimate, but I have always found parents to glow with pride at my expressions of admiration of the baby's beauty and at the resemblances to them that I can discern. They know, just as I do, that sharing their baby's photo with me is the only opportunity I have to "meet" the baby in order to witness, in a concrete way, the great love they have for their child.

Similarly, many parents are very touched when friends, family members and coworkers ask to see photos of their baby.

*Nathalie.* "I wanted to share photos and liked it when people asked to see them."

*Michelle & Aaron.* Along with many other couples I spoke to, Michelle and Aaron loved it when visitors "would use the baby's name, Olan".

*Amanda & Tim.* Using a different approach, they do not wait for people to ask about their son, Jonah. Instead, they bring him up in the conversation. "We bring him up. *So, Jonah…*, and you can tell people sometimes feel uncomfortable and think, *How do I get out of this?* We proactively set the expectation with our community that we want them to talk about Jonah and get to know our son by asking us about him. We want the opportunity to say his name and tell his story. It is still hard for us, too, but he is our son and we treasure when people ask us about him."

*Amandine & Shahrukh.* Modeling to their friends and family about how to talk about their son, Tino, was important. Amandine said, "They were relieved to follow our lead when we talked about Tino. I loved it when my friends asked lots of details about him. My mom even gave him a nickname, as you do for a live baby. It was heartwarming. We want people to use our baby's name and to remember he was our first born." A close friend said to me, 'I feel as if I met him when you talked about him.'" Amandine's aunt, going a step further, told her that the card with Tino's handprints was a gift to all the family. The aunt said, "This little boy was so wanted and we will keep him in our memory forever."

## Other Helpful Actions & Words

After some time had passed, Nidhi posted the following on Instagram to educate people on how to support a grieving person. Seven things to say or text to a grieving loved one:

- I'm sorry for your loss. It's simple but effective when you don't know what else to say. It expresses sympathy and care for the grieving loved one.

- I'm thinking about you and your family. Letting them know they are not alone and that they are in your thoughts is very comforting to the grieving loved one. If it's a baby loss, mention the baby's name.

- I can't imagine what you're going through. I'm here for you. If you haven't experienced the exact same tragedy, please admit that. Being available to them is also one of the best ways to help.

- It's horrible what you're going through. I also went through this. I'm here if you ever want to talk. Showing you are someone they can relate to is priceless and less isolating for them.

- I can only imagine how hard this must be for you. I love you. Be honest and let them know they are loved and cared for.

- I can come sit with you if you want to talk, or sit in silence. I'm here whenever you're ready, even if that's a year from now. Let them know you understand their grief has no limit.

- How can I help you? Sometimes being honest and letting them take the lead is helpful. Please don't be disappointed if they can't provide concrete ways for them to help. More likely than not, they themselves don't know how they can be helped.

Nidhi's posts on social media certainly serve the purpose of educating her community on how to support a grieving person. In addition, her more personal comments address her *biggest fear,* that her son would be forgotten by extended family and friends. "I did not want to feel that my pregnancy did not count, that my child did not count. Recently I realized that people will forget him if I let them. I will continue talking about him, posting about him on social media, writing about him. People will see him and won't have an option to forget about him."

In anticipation of their community's response to their loss, Mandy and Sean emailed a list of "helpful" actions:

- Acknowledging that this is a tragedy.
- Writing a physical letter we can read and turn to for strength (not just for sympathy).
- Waiting for us to ask for your touch or hug even when you first see us.
- Doing a chore while here (taking out trash, doing and folding laundry, watering plants, doing the dishes, etc...)

## Advice to Family and Friends of What to Avoid

### Expecting a Response

In the beginning stages of the grief, parents need to cocoon at home and keep their world very small, something I often give them permission to do. Alex and Joel felt this way for a long time. Alex said, "Our universe became very small. We felt very protective, scared, so vulnerable. Some people did not understand we needed to stay quiet. Previously we had been the kind of people who always reached out to people when they had a tough time but, when things were hard for us, we didn't have the energy or desire to cry on someone's shoulder. Some friends were offended that we did not respond to messages, but we just couldn't. I wish people would understand that and make the effort to connect with you when you are ready instead of being offended that we did not."

## Ignoring Grieving Couples

Some other people, instead of messaging their friends and relatives, sometimes stay away, either out of their deep discomfort with this kind of loss or because they fear that saying something is somehow going to make the pain worse. Some fear that mentioning the loss of the baby may be an unwelcome reminder.

Parents need validation of their pain and loss from others. One could never "remind" parents of their loss. They live it in every fiber of their being every second, minute and hour of each day. Not having their pain mentioned makes parents feel invalidated. Being ignored made Nathalie feel "angry and upset." She said, "I would have rather had people say the wrong thing rather than say nothing. And I felt invisible. Even my mom didn't want to ask questions for fear that it would upset me."

Justyna, whose family lives in Poland, said, "I was very surprised my Polish family had not said anything after we lost Matteo. But my mom told them what I needed, and my cousins and aunt reached out the next day. We had to guide them to support us."

## Invalidating the Baby's Existence

Because so little is known about the feelings associated with losing a baby during pregnancy, too many people assume the sadness can be remedied by a new pregnancy, as if babies were replaceable.

*Nathalie & Carl.* After a heart-wrenching decision to terminate the pregnancy in the second trimester when they found out their baby had severe genetic abnormalities, the couple said, "We wanted people to understand this was a real baby to us."

*Christine & André.* "People would say, *You're young, stay strong, you'll have another one.* But we lost our child! A lot of people think you'll just get pregnant again and it will be okay. They don't understand stillbirth and assume this child never existed, that there was no attachment there because you didn't know the child."

*Ryan.* "When you're vulnerable you have no protective shell. I'm usually a very tough person and I usually don't care what people think of me but, in that situation, things that I would usually handle fine just ended up scarring me.

You don't want to hear that, because you did not know your baby, you'll get over it quickly."

Most couples have told me that from the moment a wanted pregnancy takes hold, parents are eager to learn everything they can about their baby. Once mothers feel their baby move inside their body, and learn to recognize kicking and sleeping patterns, they get to know their child, even assign personalities to them *(he was so active!)*, all of which helps with attachment to this particular baby. Furthermore, both parents start imagining a future with this child—seeing their baby's first smile, watching them take their first steps, taking them to school for the first time, and passing on their values to them. They often envision their child to be by their side when they die. With a loss of a baby, a whole future disappears with that child.

## Comparing Losses & Giving Advice

Many other parents reported that friends who, upon hearing the story of the loss, would chime in with, *I know someone…*and reveal unsolicited details about another person's loss story.

*Amanda.* "This is not tit for tat—people do this like a gut reaction to show they understand, but each loss is unique and we didn't want to hear other people's stories when ours was so overwhelming."

*Sophie.* "Unless you have gone through it, and even if they have gone through it, it is such a unique loss, so they have no way of empathizing."

Other friends and relatives, in an effort to help, give advice or even criticize the way a bereaved parent is grieving.

*Christie.* "Some people put their feelings onto you or their opinions about what you should be doing. People give advice but they don't really consider what your feelings are, or listen well. Or they assume they know how you feel or what you should do."

## Dismissing Long-Term Grief

Nidhi, who grew up in India but has now lived in the United States for several years, has been very vocal about the ways she honors her son, Kian, in her daily life, and how she continues to "mother" him. She has been very brave in posting about her attempts to create a new relationship with him after he died, but has sometimes been quite hurt by reactions from friends in India who, possibly out of a different cultural attitude about death, see her as being stuck, and urge her to move on and not post about her son. In spite of her hurt, Nidhi has responded assertively on social media:

> *Just because I advocate for grief does not mean I'm "stuck." Grief is constantly transforming, but my love for Kian remains constant. My grief is valid, my role as a mother is valid, and my child is, most especially, valid.*

## Talking About the Joys & Challenges of Parenting

Many parents have expressed the desire that their friends monitor how much they talk about their fun with their own children. They know their friends do not intend to hurt them, but would like them to understand how painful it is for them to be reminded of the extent of their loss. They ask their friends to refrain from such conversations in front of them in the first few months after the loss.

Nidhi asked friends to refrain from such conversations. She said, "It was very hard in the initial phase to hear people talk about their babies and all the things they were doing that we would never get to do with Kian, like taking the kids on a trip, to the beach, or to the snow... It would be nice if people understood the things you could not do, and refrain from telling those stories. Just like our son's lack of presence is a part of our lives, they have a right to talk about their children's presence in theirs, but it would be good if they understood the impact of their words initially and were more sensitive towards our situation."

Similarly, bereaved parents find it very difficult to hear parents complain about the challenging parts of parenting, such as lack of sleep, freedom, and social life. These "stories from the front" as one mother put it, from temper tantrums to juggling the work life/family balance—are frustrating to hear. Each time they hear their friends complain, these couples feel like shouting, *I would give anything to have those problems if only my child was alive and well.*

## Asking Probing Questions

Lastly, many couples dread the avalanche of questions regarding the circumstances of the loss and recommend their friends do not ask probing questions, such as *What was wrong with the baby? Why did the doctor wait so long to induce you? What did the genetic testing reveal?* Or, *What were the results of the autopsy?*

Sara and Jay took a very proactive stance and wrote group emails to the communities they were a part of including family, friends, and colleagues at work so when they eventually faced them, they would know the story in general terms and would refrain from asking additional questions.

## Other Unhelpful Actions & Words

Emily remembered items given to her that she did not know what to do with. She said, "I have come to believe that sending flowers is one of the worst things you can do. They just die and you have to dispose of them. I was also given memorial gifts like jewelry that I would not have chosen. I appreciated the sentiment but wondered what to do with them. On the other hand, one friend asked if I wanted a piece of jewelry and, if so, did I want Juliet's name on it or all the kids' initials? That was done better and was very thoughtful."

Family and friends sometimes try to cheer the parents up by saying, *This wasn't meant to be. God needed him more.* Or, *Your father in heaven was lonely and needed her by his side.* Nidhi and Venkat heard similar comments after losing Kian. *You guys are really strong. Kian is in a better place. This is God's will. Things happen for the best.*

In a similar vein, Sean said to me so clearly, "Friends and family try to make you feel better and try to reframe the situation to find a silver lining. There is nothing you wanted about losing a child and nothing will make this hardship positive. There is nothing you can do to make this better—all you can do is listen to what people say they want." In addition, once they learned what actions and words felt hurtful to them, Mandy and Sean emailed this list to their community:

- Asking what/why/how did this happen/details—it's a sacred story we are holding.
- Saying, *Don't worry, you'll have a baby/children someday.*
- Changing the topic/cracking a joke to cheer us up. We are grieving, deeply grieving.

- Giving Mandy a hug. People often come into the room and are on the verge of crying. To say they are sorry, they often hug me. But it feels like I end up consoling them. All my touch instincts are cravings to hold Jack, not console or be consoled by others.

- Bringing clutter into the house (we just purged and nested the house to live here healthfully - no gifts, alcohol, junk food, flowers or trinkets, please.)

- Texts, emails, calls to check in—we want to reach out, not get overwhelmed.

# Answering the Questions of Strangers

## Do You Have Kids?

Bereaved parents expect comments and questions from their community of friends and family. However, those same questions are often quite jarring when they come from a stranger or from someone you know casually in a grocery store. Someone may have seen a woman grow as she advanced in her pregnancy and, after an absence from the store, ask a mother, *How is the baby? Is it a boy or a girl?* Since these questions often come up unexpectedly, and in a public place, they can be hugely triggering and make the parent feel like "a deer in the headlights."

In my work with these couples, I often recommend they have something ready to say, almost a mantra they have rehearsed at home which then feels almost like an automatic response. It can be something short and general that does not invite additional questions. Depending on how they feel that day or who their audience is, they can decide to say, *Unfortunately our baby died.* Or, *Something went wrong and we lost our baby.* Or even, *We're very sad that our baby died and are not ready to talk about it.*

*Katy & Lance.* Soon after losing their baby, Dominic, Katy remembers walking with Lance. Being postpartum, she had not yet lost her baby weight. She said, "A woman approached me and asked, 'Are you preggers?' I was caught off guard and said I had been until a couple weeks ago. What is the etiquette for this? One of your pieces of advice was to have a reason ready. Over time I've been able to say a bit more. Being more straightforward is helpful. People ask how many kids you have. It's so tricky. I say three, then they ask how old they are. If I never see them again, I say two. If I will see them again, I say, *We had three, two are alive.* It took a while not to feel guilty not counting Dominic, wanting to acknowledge him."

*Sophie.* "It still comes up that people I knew vaguely ask, *Didn't you have a baby?* Every single time the question comes up, I think, *Do I tell them or not?* I've told bus drivers, once a massage therapist—I just follow my intuition."

*Michelle & Aaron.* "Having something to say, something prepared, helped me to switch to how I was thinking about things," Aaron said. It put more focus on how I was feeling than making people comfortable. I realized this was a very painful kind of loss, and you're always a bereaved parent afterwards. So, as you answer these casual questions, they get to something really painful in ways people did not understand. I had to reflect on myself and what I needed at every step."

Michelle said, "Even now people ask, *Do you have any kids?* You have to decide what to tell to whom. It doesn't feel great not to explain but, out of self-preservation, I don't say much. With people you're going to interact with more, I say more."

## Is This Your First?

*Is this your first?* As innocent as they may sound, answers to this question are so complex that they have a great emotional impact on the parent. For a pregnant woman who has lost a precious baby, *Is this your first?* is painful, not because the question is too personal, but because the inner dialogue in the parent's head is overwhelming. One mother said, "If I say, *I don't have kids* or *this is my first,* it will feel like a lie. If I say, *I have/had one child,* they may ask the follow-up question, *How old is he/she?* And I will have to say, *He would be three in August but he died,* which will prompt, *Oh, I'm so sorry,* which will be awkward and I may have to comfort this stranger. And what happens if the person asks how my child died? What if I had to terminate the pregnancy because my baby was not viable, do I want to expose myself to a possible judgment?"

At the end of the day, even if one is prepared with a practiced statement, it may all come down to what the bereaved parent feels capable of handling emotionally in that moment. And, as I have learned in supporting bereaved parents, it is not so much whether they have a family of two or three children, some living and others gone too soon, but it is that every child counts, regardless of how long they lived, whether parents were able to meet them or why they are gone.

*        *        *

It can be very scary to approach a close friend or relative who has just lost a baby. Most people are terrified of saying the wrong thing, or expect of themselves that they should find the perfect words to lessen the pain. In fact, in dealing with grieving parents, less is more. What they most need is the warm presence of someone who can listen when they feel like talking, or be silent when they don't, someone who can hear the worst of their thoughts or tolerate their most intense feelings without pointing to anything positive about the loss or trying to fix the pain—basically someone who understands this grief will last a very long time and who can take the lead of the grieving parent. Concrete actions like bringing food without expecting a conversation, or babysitting the couple's other children, can also be very helpful. In addition, since a lot of couples fear their baby will be forgotten, or that people don't understand their love and attachment to a baby that did not live, it is important for family and friends to say the baby's name and to bring the child up into conversations.

It is also very meaningful to these couples when their community understands they need space in the initial phase of the grief so they are not offended when they do not receive a response to messages or gifts. At the same time, being ignored makes couples feel invisible, so it can be challenging for family and friends to navigate the line between giving space and offering a gentle presence. This challenge can be remedied by asking *How are you doing today?* Or, *What do you need from me today?* Parents also like it when people around them understand their loss was unique to them and therefore not having it compared to other losses. In dealing with strangers' questions about the loss, parents find it very helpful to be prepared with a short, general response which acknowledges the baby's death without inviting additional questions. Lastly, because the parents long for the particular baby that died, it does not help to hear that having another baby will make them feel better—babies are not replaceable.

Maybe family and friends will better understand the depth of this kind of loss through the words of one bereaved parent: *The shadows they cast, the holes they leave in us, it all counts.*

# SEVEN

# Grieving Styles and Learning to Work as a Team

*I had been trying to give her what I needed, and she had been trying to give me what she needed.*

– Robert

*We learned about each other and how to respect our different reactions.*

– Justyna

IN THE FIRST FEW WEEKS AFTER LOSING A BABY, couples are often extremely united. They have gone from experiencing the joy of expecting a baby to the somber reality of their baby's death. They may have agonized over the decision to end a pregnancy because their baby was not viable or they may have delivered a stillborn baby. Other couples may have learned after birth their baby would soon die. Even if family and friends have gathered to support them, they are the only ones who remember every second of this nightmarish reality.

Having witnessed the next phase of grief many times, I prepare couples for the eventuality that individual grief reactions may emerge and which may be different from their partner's.

Grief theorists have emphasized that there are many ways people grieve but that there is a continuum of grief with two different patterns on either end—"intuitive" versus "instrumental" grieving styles.[24] Intuitive grievers, often stereotyped as female, tend to experience their grief in a highly emotional way whereas instrumental grievers, often stereotyped as male, cope by focusing on practical matters and problem-solving. Rarely is someone exclusively intuitive or instrumental. Most people actually display a blend of both styles.

It is important for partners to accept that these different grieving styles are a reflection of their own nature, not an expression of "not grieving right." For example, a mother who does not see her partner cry, but watches him engage instead in practical tasks, may conclude that he is not suffering the loss of their baby as much as she is. Similarly, a father who sees his partner crying day after day, week after week, may fear she will never return to her previous self. In addition, since he has an instinct to fix problems, he may end up feeling helpless and unable to protect his partner. Because both partners are feeling so raw, they often don't have the emotional bandwidth or perspective to accept that they are each doing the best they can in grieving according to their own nature. The conclusions reached are often that one partner is "over-emotional" and the other "in denial" or "unfeeling." This can lead to parents feeling very lonely and for divisions between them to create tension in their relationship.

Having observed these differences in grieving styles frequently, and the assumptions made as a result, I gently guide couples to respect their partners' nature and to learn to work better as a team. Many couples voice a fear that this tragedy will lead them to break up. Even though the literature and common belief tend to perpetuate the myth that couples who lose a baby have a high likelihood of divorcing, the research has not found any convincing evidence to corroborate this belief, which is something I share with the couples I see in counseling.[25] What seems to be true instead is that a pre-existing high level of marital satisfaction leads to the least amount of conflict among bereaved couples.[26] Regardless of the quality of the parents' relationship, I have found it useful to ask them about the story of their relationship—how they fell in love and what qualities they appreciate in each other. I remind them of their bond as a couple before they decided to build a family together and I highlight the resources they can now draw upon.

# Mothers' Voices

*Nathalie.* "When Carl went back to work, we went all of a sudden to feeling disconnected at a time I needed so badly to feel connected. I saw him as hiding his feelings, and I wanted to say, *How are you fine when I'm wallowing in grief?* I felt envious that he had a job where he could feel distracted when I couldn't do that."

*Sara.* "I felt disconnected from Jay. It was very hard for quite a while. Jay coped by *doing*—building things, hiking, acting as if he could cope—and I felt he did not understand my pain or was feeling it."

*Michelle.* "We were in different places when Aaron went back to work. I went really deep into my grief, and it was really hard to see him functioning well. He was needing to not share his grief with everybody to protect himself. Once I said to Aaron 'I feel you don't remember him every day. I want you to look through Olan's chest (where his mementos are kept) and take a moment.' It was sort of demanding on my part, but that's what I needed so that he would step into the grief. It was more about me, and what I needed, not taking into account what he needed."

*Amandine.* "When Shahrukh went back to work, he talked about being excited about our new apartment and I was home and crying and telling him, 'How can you be excited?' He was doing better, finding excitement about things, and we fought because I was still crying five weeks later, and he was not. All I could think of was that every day that passed was one more day I no longer had with my baby. I was locked in my grief, suffering so much, and noticed how we did not cope the same way."

*Sophie.* After a while of noticing Ryan being less emotional than she was she finally confronted him and said, 'Are you even sad? Are you over this? You are the only person who is grieving what I am grieving, but it doesn't seem like you are.'

*Lena.* Needing to see some emotion in her husband, Luis, after they lost their daughter, she said, "As women we see that men are conditioned to be tough and not cry. For me, tears need to come out. I told him it's okay to cry, and he did. I'm so grateful that he could do that."

*Christie.* Some mothers felt they disappointed their husbands by not having a successful pregnancy. Christie shared this with me and her husband, Wayne,

"It was hard for me to talk to him because I felt I let him down. It was my job to take care of the baby and my body had failed him. I also felt guilty because I had wanted a child more than he did. So, after pushing him so much to get pregnant, I couldn't carry this baby. I couldn't talk to Wayne because of my insecurity and because I was afraid he would agree with me that it was my fault."

*Christine.* When her own highs and lows did not coincide with her husband's, she felt frustrated. "We would take turns. I'd be having a really tough one to two weeks and wanted him with me. Then I'd come out of it and he was having a tough time. It was frustrating as a scenario not to overlap. But it was also nice to be there for each other."

*Katherine.* George's fortitude was a source of great comfort to her after they lost Neil. "I really appreciated how calm my husband was at the worst of times. He showed a lot of strength when we learned our son would not survive. You really need to understand each other. Some people may do crazy things while learning to cope, so you really have to support each other as a couple."

In addition, Katherine accepted that she and George had different coping styles. "George liked to spend time by himself. He didn't need to talk with people, so he kept himself busy watching online news, listening to the radio. And he made a frame of Neil's photo. He grieved in his own way. But I needed to talk with people who had had similar experiences. I also had a friend from church who had the exact same issue, so it was good to talk with her. I had a hard time looking at photos of Neil whereas George needed to look at them. Even five years later, I can't. I think about him, and will always love him, but I can't bear looking at the photos, even now, five years later."

*Nidhi.* Although Venkat's coping style was different from hers, she did not find this difference to be challenging. Nidhi said, "Venkat wants to talk about his feelings, but he finds it hard to do. Instead he needs to be active and feel it in his body, by going biking or swimming—that's what brings him support. It's just his way of coping and it does not mean he doesn't care about Kian. I feel very supported by Venkat. He's the person I feel the most comfortable and safe with to talk about my feelings of anger, sorrow, and all the different types of emotions."

The comments made by the women I interviewed were similar to those I have heard from many mothers over the years. Many women would like their partners to express their sadness over the loss of their baby more openly.

When the fathers appear energized by the return to work, or able to engage in tasks, they often tend to interpret this behavior as evidence their suffering is less intense than theirs. In addition, many women carry a sense of failure and guilt over their baby's death, and sometimes fear their husbands may hold them responsible. Because these women feel so vulnerable, they find it very hard to ask for what they need.

Yet other mothers note and accept their partners' different grieving style without making assumptions about the intensity of their pain, and even appreciate how they complement each other. Some other mothers wish their husbands' high and low points would coincide with theirs, but also concede that it is helpful to be able to pull each other out of sadness when one of them feels stronger. Regardless of women's individual grieving styles, what is helpful over time is for them to be open and honest about their needs. In addition, when a partner says or does something they find hurtful, it is important for them to remain in conversation with their partners and to refrain from making assumptions.

## Fathers' Voices

*Ryan.* Focused on supporting his wife, he kept his grief private at times. "When I go running I talk to Spencer. Sometimes, at home, I cuddle her stuffed bunny, say hello to it. But I didn't tell Sophie I was doing that because this was my private way of grieving. Those things I was doing alone—I didn't want to brag about it to Sophie. What helped me was to be strong for her. I wanted to be supportive of her, but when I was alone I could be sad."

*Carl.* Protective, as well, of Nathalie's feelings, he kept his emotions to himself. "I did not express my emotions because I did not want to make it harder for her. I was trying to help her, which was a problem for us and caused some conflict. I had always been able to make things work out, but here there was nothing I could do. Afterwards, I tried hard to rebuild that internal confidence in myself."

*Adrien.* Unable to find a solution to Justyna's sorrow caused him to struggle greatly. "I wanted to help, but that was not what she needed. Usually I see a problem and look for a solution. But, in this case, no solution I came up with was valued or helpful, so that was frustrating. So I felt isolated and so did she."

*Aaron.* Processing his feelings privately is consistent with his nature. "I'm a lot more into processing internally rather than talking about things. I can figure them out in my head and then come together for a conversation. It's part of my issue of not putting something out there that's not completely thought through."

*Joel.* After he voiced his hopelessness about their future, he said, "I didn't know how I was processing. I couldn't label my emotions and put them into words. What I was unable to express was that there would be pain for us for the rest of our lives, that a part of us would always be missing."

*Luis.* At times, he also had a hard time expressing his emotions. "It was easier for Lena to release and let go of her emotions, whereas I thought, 'I don't need to do this.' I felt she had a better grasp on how to manage and handle her emotions."

*Robert.* With fear that he was bottling up his emotions, Rebecca needed him to talk. Robert had another explanation. He said, "It's easier on me to not dwell on those feelings whereas for Rebecca, it's important for her to do that because that is how she is processing. I did not need to talk about it very much. She felt that, if I was not doing it her way, I was not doing it right. So I was relieved she had a place to do that in counseling."

*Wayne.* Surprised to hear that Christie felt she had failed him by not having a successful pregnancy, he struggled with ways to help her. "I would never have felt she had failed me. I was more afraid that I couldn't give her what she wanted after losing the baby. The hardest thing was not to try to fix her pain—to resist being overbearing and telling her what to do—and just listen instead."

Other men felt the reality of not having carried the baby created a different experience between them and their partners.

*André.* "Internally it's not the same. Christine was with Isla for eight months, twenty-four hours a day. I would talk to the baby and feel her kick, but dads can't miss the past relationship with the baby in the same way as the moms. It brings up guilt when your partner feels so sad and you don't have the same level of sadness. You're also in a dark hole, and I tried to share the dark space with Christine, but it's a different hole and experience."

*Lance.* "Katy was much more struck by grief. Hers was much more raw than mine. She's more emotional than me and she carried and nourished the baby. I did not feel the same intimacy and connection. The way I emote is also very different. I'm just not as expressive as Katy is. The loss of a child is the loss of an entire future—playing catch, pushing the child on the swings, the first day of school, graduation...I did not think about those during the pregnancy, but I really did afterwards."

Again, the fathers I interviewed confirmed what other men have shared with me in the past. Many fathers have different needs and experiences from their partners. Whereas women often express a need to witness their partners' sadness and hear them verbalize it so as to feel connected to them, many men find it more comfortable to grieve on their own. Sometimes this is because they tend to process in private. For many bereaved men, their partners' intense emotions makes them feel both protective and terrified, and they become intent on finding solutions to relieve their pain. By contrast, what most women want is to be held and for their husbands to listen to their thoughts and fears and demonstrate they can tolerate their tears.

# How Couples Worked on Their Grief

## Honest Communication

Some couples started to talk openly after losing their baby about their commitment to being honest with each other and strengthening their bond.

*Amanda & Tim.* Working as a team before and after Jonah died was a commitment they made to each other during their time in the NICU. Tim said, "I know some couples blame each other and drift apart, but we did not do that. This was not a burden we had to carry alone. We said it was our biggest fear, and we vocalized it." Amanda said, "When Jonah was in the NICU, I said to Tim, 'The only thing worse than losing Jonah would be to lose you too.' We had that conversation before he passed away. I'm proud we acknowledged it, so that when we had those bad days, we did not take it out on each other. We did everything as a team."

*Michelle & Aaron.* Since they had been a couple for a long time before getting pregnant, Michelle and Aaron called on the foundation of their relationship. Michelle said, "One of the strengths of our relationship is that we're open with each other. That's the basis of our relationship. Day by day we shared how we were feeling. When we were not on the same page, we would say, 'I feel differently from you today'—doing our best to be honest with the fact that we were not always going through the exact same thing."

*Alex & Joel.* As they began to face the deep pain of losing Hunter, they leaned on the strength of their relationship. Alex said, "We'd always had a strong bond. We appreciate the love we have for each other. We wanted to talk about our love, how we met, our marriage, what brought Hunter to fruition. We needed to express that to each other. She came from our love. That brought a small amount of light to our situation. Our love was going to keep things growing in the right direction." Joel said, "We never shrank from our emotions. We made a very conscious effort to face our emotions and that really helped us. We were afraid it would drive us apart, but we were not willing to blame the person closest to us. We went the complete opposite direction and stayed close. It actually brought us closer."

*Rebecca & Robert.* Communicating honestly was their priority. Rebecca said, "We had to up our communication game. When I was talking to Robert about strong feelings and it became too much, we had to communicate that to each other. Robert did not use to be able to express it when he was upset, but now he can identify it and say, 'It's hard to hear about this right now.' Instead of shutting down, we figured a way to listen to each other and also put a stop to it when needed." Robert said, "I got better at validating instead of fixing. You can't fix losing a child."

## Seeking Support Outside the Couple

Over time many parents started to feel comfortable going outside their relationship for support. They realized that a woman who had lost a baby under similar circumstances might best understand their feelings. Sometimes they felt even better supported by virtue of being women. Many mothers sought out the company of other "loss moms" through friends, on Facebook, or other online platforms. Having their wives receive support from sources other than themselves was often a bit of a relief for the men who felt stretched by their return to work and different approach to grief.

For example, when Amanda got pregnant again after losing Jonah, she "spent a lot of time with another mom who had lost a baby and was also pregnant." She said, "It was so special having a fellow mom who understood the complicated joy of welcoming a baby after losing one." Their friendship continued through their pregnancies and the arrival of their babies.

Sophie found that "finding somebody else outside of your partner can be hugely helpful." In addition, she and Ryan benefited from spending time with another couple. "We had a friend who connected us to a couple who had lost a baby. We met them about two weeks after we lost Spencer. They had a two-year-old, and that gave us hope that there can be hope after this."

Many couples, out of fear they might drift apart, commit early on to working toward an honest communication. They find it very helpful to acknowledge their individual needs and reactions without blaming each other and to validate their partners' emotions instead of offering solutions. Couples learn to expect that they will grieve differently at times, and be more in line with each other's grief needs at other times. They also find great support in other parents who have suffered similar losses, whether individually as many women do, or as couples. Life has dealt them a huge blow, but it can be important to remember they are the only two people who can make their relationship survive and, possibly, even grow.

# How Counseling Helped

## Validation

After losing a baby, couples are confronted with a crisis they never anticipated or could prepare for, and they need help navigating an unknown and terrifying territory. Their minds and hearts keep returning to the moment the baby died, in an effort to both comprehend the reality of the tragedy, but also to hold onto the last living memories of their child. The emotions that accompany this initial period of the grief often lead them to feel and act in ways that are foreign to themselves and to their partners. They often fear they will never return to their old, capable, and well-functioning ways.

By learning in counseling that their reactions are natural under the circumstances, and common to many parents who lose a baby, couples receive both validation of their feelings and much-needed reassurance that they are behaving as expected.

*Alex.* "We didn't know how to navigate this. We knew we couldn't do this on our own. Talking to someone who came to our home, understood us, listened to us, and helped guide us in the most challenging time of our lives was a lifeline. Hearing from someone who had spoken to many bereaved parents that our feelings were normal brought us huge relief. It was also something we could share with people in our lives, that we were not strange and needed to go through this."

*Wayne.* "When I complained about being so tired, I remember you telling me, *This is a normal part of the grieving process.* And a light went off in my head and I could tell myself there was nothing wrong with me. I was supposed to feel this way, and I was going to be okay. It also changed the way I was going to talk to Christie, and learn to just hold her when she was upset instead of trying to fix things. For us, talking in counseling was an investment in each other, and gave us some real quality time afterward to talk and spend together."

*Sophie.* Through counseling, normalizing feelings was a step towards healing. "It helped to understand how other women go through this kind of loss, and validate that what Ryan was feeling was normal and I should not worry about it too much."

*Amandine.* Hearing other women's reactions to grief was comforting. "Hearing about other people's experience, and that my reaction was normal, was so reassuring. I could tell Shahrukh what you said, and it helped us so much to better understand each other and to know I was not going crazy."

## Working Through Grieving Differences

*Sara & Jay.* Reporting that he felt much closer to Sara after counseling, Jay said, "It was only after we met with you and heard how common it is for couples to grieve differently that we started to respect our respective ways of coping. Over time, Sara started to be able to function, and I was reassured that she would eventually be okay."

*Justyna & Adrien.* "We learned about each other and to respect our different reactions," Adrien said. "We started to communicate differently, and it brought us closer." Justyna said, "I did not realize there could be such a different way of reacting. Counseling led us toward each other and to talking together."

*Rebecca & Robert.* Relieved after learning about grieving differences during counseling, Robert said, "You told us to respect our differences in grieving, and that was very helpful. I had been trying to give her what I needed, and she had been trying to give me what she needed." Rebecca said, "We talked a lot about our differences as a couple, and we were determined it was not going to break us up. If we were having a disagreement, we talked very openly about that. "

*Nathalie & Carl.* Witnessing the emerging differences between her grieving style and Carl's, Nathalie said, "At the beginning we were the closest we'd ever been. When you said it might change, it was so helpful because it did change, and it was good to know it was common."

"I was afraid at one point that I was going to push Carl away with my sadness. I remember going through a period of being afraid of losing everybody. In working with you, we ended up talking to each other about what we were each doing. Then we could be more open and we could understand each other even if we were in different places. And I was relieved that I was not going to drive him away with my sadness."

*Sophie & Ryan.* Counseling created a structure to have conversations they might not have had on their own. Sophie said, "Sometimes when we met, you would say, 'Sophie, why don't you tell Ryan how you think about this,' or 'Ryan, what do you think about this?' It was almost as if, hearing somebody else say it feels less scary than bringing it up on our own."

Sophie added, "I know the value of therapy, and I think having someone who is trained and knows the right questions was very helpful. We would recommend it to other couples who go through this even if they have reservations about it. You start talking more openly about your feelings. You realize you are together in this but are affected differently, and then you come back together to remind yourselves that you are together in this. We learned to take the time to discuss our feelings with each other."

\*    \*    \*

After losing a baby, couples are often confronted with their own intense feelings, as well as those of their partners. They may never have experienced or witnessed these feelings in each other. This can give rise to fears that their reactions may not be normal or that the other person will never be able to function. It is therefore very important for a counselor to both validate these strong emotions as being expected after this kind of loss, and to inform them that they are not alone and within the range of normal behavior. At many times during the grieving process I normalize whatever feelings parents share with me as well as my experience with others.

In addition, couples find it helpful to learn that they may have different grief reactions as they re-engage with life, which is very common. Counseling creates both a safe place and a structure to speak openly, to hear the other parent, and to express some of the fears that may arise. It can also be an opportunity for the counselor to model how to respond to strong feelings and respect differences in an atmosphere of acceptance. As the counselor guides couples patiently and with empathy through the uncharted territory of this profound loss, they often realize they have an opportunity to strengthen their relationship.

# EIGHT

# Examples of Rituals and Places to Honor Babies

*We are making new memories in his name.*
*It's not the same as making memories with him*
*but it's all we have.*

— Nidhi and Venkat

MANY GRIEF THEORISTS TALK ABOUT the importance of maintaining a dynamic and ongoing connection to the person who has died, a concept called "Continuing Bonds"[27] or "Loving in Separation"[28], which brings great comfort to the bereaved. This important phase of the grief process moves the griever from "loving in presence" to "loving in absence" and allows a grieving parent to hold onto the tie to their baby as it transforms over time.[29] Some observers might think this is a form of denial but, as I have often observed, developing rituals to honor their baby allows the parents to mark important dates and to incorporate their baby's memory while reinvesting in life.

Without any prompting on my part, I have witnessed countless examples of creative and inspiring ways bereaved parents memorialize their baby over time. It is important to note that parents, and even individuals within a couple, may feel more comfortable honoring their babies privately and not through big gestures. This should not be construed to mean that they love their children any less, just as a reflection of their nature. Just as grief is as unique as the couples affected by it, the examples below reflect their distinctive love for their baby and what brings them solace.

# Significant Dates

## The Due Date

Couples who lose their baby before their due date find this day, marked from the first doctor's visit, to be especially painful without a baby in their arms.

Amandine and Shahrukh, who were told that their baby, Tino, had died during the second trimester, celebrated his due date in their own special way. They took a cake to the beach, brought the urn containing Tino's ashes, had a picnic, gathered seaweed (which represented Amandine's work as a marine biologist) onto the sand, and watched the waves sweep them out to sea.

Nathalie and Carl tragically lost their baby in the second trimester of pregnancy. They had been grieving privately for weeks but refused to let the due date pass without an acknowledgment of their son's existence. I was moved by their courage when Nathalie posted this message on social media:

> *Too often this kind of loss is a silent story, but we decided to share that today was supposed to be our baby's due date. We love you so much, Sam.*

When I spoke with Nathalie and Carl they had welcomed a baby girl into their family. Nathalie said, "I remember the need for Sam to be known, and I felt like I would be betraying him with a future child if I had not acknowledged him at all. So many people reached out to me privately and were so thankful I was open about it. It angers me there is so much silence around this type of loss."

Many mothers feel like their children are still a part of them long after they have given birth. Biologists have found evidence of this phenomenon.[30] During pregnancy, some of the fetus's cells leave the womb, traveling through the placenta and into the mother's bloodstream, where they end up in various parts of her body. The mother's body kills off most of these circulating fetal cells shortly after pregnancy. But some evade the immune system and can stay for long periods of time in the mother's body. In some cases even a lifetime, according to these biologists. This might explain why, after losing a baby, some mothers experience the due date in a physical way, almost as if their body was holding their sadness and prompting them to pay special attention to it.

Rebecca, who lost her son mid-pregnancy, said, "On his due date I did not feel good, and the next day I remembered it was that day. His DNA is still inside me." Many mothers find great comfort in knowing they may keep some of their baby's cells inside them for a very long time.

## Birthdays

*Lena & Luis.* Six days after her birth, they lost their daughter, Nayeli. Lena said, "Last year, we celebrated Nayeli's birthday. We took a picture of a piñata, got some pan dulce, put a small offering on her altar, and had sparklers."

Luis teared up and said, "When we sign cards, we sign with a star—she is always going to be a part of our family's signature."

*Alex & Joel.* It took a full year before they could speak publicly about their beloved daughter, Hunter, stillborn at thirty-eight weeks of gestation. I had been an eyewitness to their raw pain for a very long time and observed their tentative but growing need to share their deep love for their daughter with their community.

On the first year anniversary of her birth Alex and Joel posted the following message on Facebook:

*Our daughter would have been one today. Instead, we celebrate without her, honoring her beautiful spirit that we believe soars the skies like a California condor. Condors are rare to spot, but they glide along the incredible California coastline and, if you're lucky enough, you can see and hear them as they catch the gusts of winds that blow along the scenic trails. Our daughter is just as rare as one of them. The weeks, months and now year after her passing have been like putting back together a million tiny shards of glass. Losing a child is the loss of a future—a future that you build for, that you try and plan for, and that you lovingly envision over the course of nine months. Joel and I had created an incredible human being that stemmed from our immense love for one another, only to have her torn away from us. Today and always, we honor Hunter—she is our guiding light, our majestic bird who soars the skies and is everything beautiful in this world. She is our inspiration, our strength, our whole heart. And though she is not with us, she will always hold a special place in our hearts and souls, and we will always be a family.*

*Mandy & Sean.* After losing their son, Jack, who was also stillborn, they marked his birthday in this manner. Sean said, "We did a family retreat around his birthday last year. We wanted to remember this baby boy as something positive, in the outdoors, going on a hike, being in this world we love so much and had wanted Jack to be a part of. We did not want to make it a day of gloom."

Mandy said, "The last day of his life was the summer solstice, which seems fitting. The next day was the day of his passing, and the day after that was the day of his birth."

She explained how they held a three-day celebration. "The first day was vitality, the second day was health—we made a commitment we were going to take good care of ourselves on the day of his passing—and the third day was his birthday, so we decided to make it fun. So we went to a baseball game, being part of many people. On the day of his passing we worked on our financial health and a family budget, and on the day of his birthday, we went on a seaplane tour, which was just fun."

*Katy & Lance.* After losing Dominic, they had two children and had to learn how to express both the sadness of the loss and their joy at having more children. Lance said, "We celebrate his birthday. He would be turning four this year, and it makes me sad. Do I love my other children any less? Of course not. But it is a paradox to think that if Dominic had not passed away, his brother would not have been conceived." Katy said, "We're the kind of people who think about things and look for explanations, but this is the kind of thing with no clear explanation. "It means a lot to us when we hear of people visiting our son in the cemetery."

Some people mark the birthday in very simple, but not less meaningful, ways. Some blow up balloons, return to the beach where the ashes were scattered, or light a candle in honor of their baby.

*Christine & André.* To remain close to their baby, Isla, who was stillborn on March 16th, they honor her every month. "Every month on the 16th we light a candle, we go to her crib and look at the items we placed there. We don't know how we'll continue. We'll still honor her birthday. This is a long-time grief. It doesn't go away. Some people are surprised we are still struggling instead of moving on from it. It makes us smile to see the picture of her hand. Our future children will know about her. We joke that our other kids are going to be out of luck - she was such a perfect child!"

*Sophie & Ryan.* After losing their daughter, Spencer, right after birth, they have kept her memory alive by giving her name as a middle name to their two subsequent children. They also celebrate their daughter's birthday each year. Sophie said, "For her first and second birthday, we asked friends to donate a toy to a shelter in her name. On her third birthday, we took our son with us to honor his older sister. We went to 'Spencer's spot'—a grove of trees where we used to go a lot. It's one of the places we plan to spread her ashes. There are dogs running and Ryan can see it from the Bay when he is sailing. This time her birthday wasn't as painful as it was a nice family moment with our new baby."

*Emily & Gerry.* After losing Juliet, they are thinking of celebrating their living twin, Clara, on her own and marking Juliet's birthday at a different time. Emily said, "Because Juliet died so close to Clara's birthday, I very much want to celebrate Clara's birthday separately from her sister. We might have a plaque in the Botanical Garden and take the kids there to play on another day, like the day we found out we were expecting twins."

## Anniversaries

Other couples feel the need to include their baby on their wedding anniversary. After Nidhi and Venkat's son, Kian, died in utero just before the due date, they created rituals to keep him in their lives as they reengaged in theirs. Nidhi said,

Figure 8.1

"On our wedding anniversary, we took his framed photo to the restaurant, had our picture taken with him, and posted it (Figure 8.1). I wanted to show people we are still alive and trying to celebrate ourselves by going out. We don't want to overshadow our lives with the death of Kian."

## Mother's Day & Father's Day

Mother's Day and Father's Day can also be a very painful time for bereaved parents. They have become mothers and fathers without a live baby by their side and, very often, they are ignored on a day when other families celebrate with special meals, cards, gifts and flowers. Many of the couples I have supported have been touched by the rare acknowledgements they have received that affirm their identity as parents and their sadness on that day. Something as simple as sending a text to bereaved mothers and fathers on that day can be very meaningful. Some parents who are further along in their grief, or have become advocates for themselves, sometimes guide their community in supporting them by posting on social media, *I miss you on Mother's Day and will always love you.*

A special day has been set aside for bereaved mothers—International Bereaved Mother's Day—on the Sunday before Mother's Day. It is a day to honor women who have lost a child in any way, including women who have lost their chance to become a mother through infertility.

## Holidays

Most parents dread the arrival of the holidays, especially the first year after losing their baby. Parents often express great sadness over not being able to celebrate religious, cultural or national holidays, including Thanksgiving, Christmas or Hanukkah, with their baby as they had looked forward to. The approach of the holiday gives rise to great anxiety and indecision about whether to mark the day or skip it all altogether. In counseling I validate these parents' feelings and allow them to brainstorm about what will decrease some of these intense emotions. Finding a bit of control at a time when they have lost so much is very helpful.

*Michelle & Aaron.* After losing Olan the day before a scheduled C-section, they thoughtfully debated whether or not to "take a year off from holidays."

They certainly did not want to travel to where they had imagined going with their baby. Instead, they invited their families to their home for Thanksgiving and asked them to cook the traditional meal so they wouldn't be overwhelmed. I thought this was a brilliant idea, one that allowed them to be comforted by their loved ones with the delicious smells of food around them, and one which allowed their families to do something concrete for their daughter and son at a time when all were mourning baby Olan.

*Amanda & Tim.* On the first holidays which fell soon after the loss of their son, Amanda said, "Jonah passed away just before Thanksgiving, and we made little photo books, full of pictures. And we brought those with us to our family—it felt like it was a piece of him we were bringing to those gatherings. We knew those pictures very well, so we got good at telling the stories we told about him, how much he liked the pool at George Mark Children's House, for example, even if people were sobbing listening to us. We wanted our families to know him and his sweet personality. He was such an incredible baby! We also have a candle that we made in memory of Jonah, so we brought the candle to the holidays with our families. Our holiday card this year had our new baby, our dog, and we signed it 'from our angel Jonah.' We wanted him to be included in the card."

## Other Ways to Honor Babies over Time

In my grief work with bereaved parents, I have noted a shift in the ways parents want to honor their babies over time. Once the anxiety over how to mark the holidays, anniversaries, or special dates like the due date fades over the first six months to a year, the parents often seek more permanent ways to memorialize their babies by planting trees, creating altars in their homes, developing rituals such as saying the baby's name when lighting a candle, as well as organizing toy drives or fundraisers as legacies for their children.

Some parents, possibly in an attempt to merge a part of their babies' bodies into their own, sometimes tattoo the baby's name or a symbol of the baby - an octopus, for example - onto their arms even mixing the tattoo ink with some of the baby's ashes.

Some others, like Christie and Wayne, chose to conserve some ashes into a special container. Christie said, "We chose the name Archer for our son because it implied strength and also an archangel as a protector. I found a memorial necklace with a pendant that felt just right (Figure 8.2). I chose an amber stone which was Archer's birthstone, since his due date was November, and asked the Neptune Society to place some of Archer's ashes into the pendant. The pendant has wings around it which felt just right. At first I was wearing the necklace all the time, wanting to feel Archer close to me but, over time, it started to feel heavy on my heart and made me sad. So now I wear him for family photos, where I always want him to be, or special events like Thanksgiving, Christmas or a birthday party. When I prepared my hospital bag to give birth to Archer's little sister, I wanted to take the pendant with me, but I was too scared to lose it and left it at home. Wayne also wanted to keep some of Archer's ashes, but he chose a round pillbox for them which he keeps in his closet next to a heart which contains his father's ashes and his wedding ring."

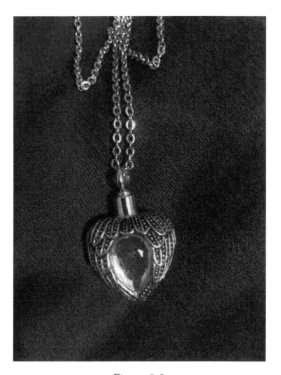

Figure 8.2

Several of the couples I have met have planted trees in their backyard or created a garden in their baby's memory. They want to see life grow out of their love for their child in a concrete way—a life to remember a life. Sara and Jay planted a pear tree in honor of their daughter, Lena (Figure 8.3).

Figure 8.3

A friend of Sara's made a bear, called "Lena Bear," with weights inside it that matched baby Lena's weight. For a very long time after they lost Lena and through a subsequent pregnancy, Sara would hug Lena Bear to her chest and take her to bed with her.

The family also carved Lena's name into a rock and placed it in their backyard (Figure 8.4).

Figure 8.4

For Carl and Nathalie, dragonflies came to represent their son, Sam. They have a drawing with Sam's name on it and dragonflies in their home and a beautiful urn with a dragonfly motif made by a woman who had made a bowl for their wedding (Figure 8.5 and Figure 8.6). Nathalie was very moved by Carl's revelation during our interview, that he touches the urn every so often to connect physically with his son.

Figure 8.5            Figure 8.6

Alex and Joel, as we learned, have chosen condors to represent their daughter, Hunter (Figure 8.7). They have expanded the concept of the condor's majesty to include all natural beauty as a symbol of their daughter.

Figure 8.7

Alex said, "When we see beauty, we think of her. She's our inspiration. When we see a beautiful sunset we think of her. Or the birds on the line. We got an ornament for her in Europe, and now we are making an ornament for each of us. We tell her we love her."

Amanda and Tim have selected whales to represent Jonah because of the story of Jonah and the whale from the Bible. Amanda said, "All over the house we have his pictures. And we have lots of whales because of the story of Jonah and the whale." Tim added, "Jonah gets eaten by a whale. It's a symbol to us of a person who went their own way, who is different from the norm, as our son was. It's helpful to have them and our friends think of Jonah when they see a whale somewhere."

Amanda and Tim started a fundraising campaign in Jonah's memory for the Child Life Program at George Mark Children's House. Tim said, "The Child Life Program at George Mark House helps families focus on living and treasuring every moment with their sick children. We started a fundraiser for the Child Life Program so that other parents could benefit from the same services. It was a very healing thing for our community to be able to donate in Jonah's honor." Amanda said, "I wear a necklace that has both of my sons' names and a blue ring that Tim gave me when Jonah was born. I love carrying Jonah with me in this way, and it is a good prompt when I want to talk about him to other people. "

**Jonah Timothy Cantwell**
October 1st, 2018 | 9 lbs. 8 Oz | 21.5 Inches

Figure 8.8                                Figure 8.9 Jonah's hand and footprints

Christine also has a new appreciation for beauty after losing her daughter, Isla. "Things are more beautiful to me. Maybe I appreciate life more. I look for connection to Isla around me—a perfect double rainbow, a hummingbird looking at me. Six months ago I felt despair. I know now we're going to have a beautiful life."

Other parents get very creative. After losing Spencer, Sophie had the inspiration to write a series of books about *Spencer's Adventures*. The books would be a collaboration between Sophie as the writer and her sister who would illustrate the books. Ryan, Spencer's father, viewed this effort as "very cathartic—to put the experience on paper."

Sophie's idea was to tell stories featuring a bunny named Spencer in honor of their daughter. "Spencer goes on an adventure and there is a silver lining. Spencer Bunny was presented with a situation, like there is a long line to get into the zoo, or it's raining outside, and Spencer Bunny would say 'let's put on rain boots and play I Spy!'. Out of a tragedy we can become stronger people." For a long time after Spencer died, Sophie slept with a bunny she had bought for her. Now Spencer's younger brother has the bunny in his room, and his newborn sister will also have a bunny in the nursery. Sophie and Ryan also placed a memory brick in Spencer's honor in their local park (Figure 8.10). Sophie said, "We wanted to have her with us when we're out enjoying our home town."

Figure 8.10

Sometimes friends and family also participate in creating a legacy. After Michelle and Aaron's son, Olan, was born still, Michelle and her mother-in-law sewed twenty white gowns with a red heart and twenty knit hats for stillborn babies and donated them to the hospital where Olan was delivered (Figure 8.11 and Figure 8.12). They made them in several sizes so that some could fit infant babies. When I saw them while visiting Michelle and Aaron, I was so moved by their generosity in wanting to give something beautiful to parents of stillborn babies. When Michelle, Aaron and Aaron's mother brought the gowns and hats to the hospital, it was an emotional return. Michelle said, "It felt a little like a graduation, or perhaps just some closure, to walk back into the hospital".

Figure 8.11

Figure 8.12

Olan was named after Aaron's grandfather. Michelle and Aaron have a chest that had belonged to Aaron's grandfather. Aaron explained the importance of the chest and some other rituals that bring him comfort. "We wanted to pull every mementos—cards, photos, footprints….At a certain point, the hand and footprints were cracking, so I had them scanned in a 3-D printer so they could last a long time, and they picked up a lot of details. We have so few things of his that it was scary to see those cracks. Because he had been inside Michelle for so long, his blood and DNA are inside her. Sometimes I put my hand on her heart to feel close to him. I also have a little felt star that was in Olan's room, and I take it with me."

Michelle said, "Friends organized a plaque at the playground Aaron designed in our neighborhood. It's been good for us. We have his ashes at home, so having a marker out in the world feels good to us. The plaque says 'For our son, Olan.' The other thing friends did was a tree planting effort—70 trees in our neighborhood. They have markers on them that say 'a tree for Olan.' That was hard for us because of its public nature. We weren't sure we were ready for it. It felt so final at first, like acknowledging our son had died. But now it feels very comforting to see people contribute to it. And it was good for the people involved as well."

Katherine and George, whose son, Neil, died of Pompe, a genetic disorder, at six months of age, felt driven to make some donations. Katherine said, "We made some donations to George Mark Children's House where he passed away, to the Association for Glycogen Storage Disease and to Stanford Children's Hospital, among others. Our older son, at the age of fifteen, also helped disabled children, mostly with autism, with art and music. He started several years ago and is still volunteering there in honor of his little brother. He is doing well there. He is very patient and it's good for him as a person to learn this."

For some couples each day brings a new opportunity to honor their baby. Nidhi and Venkat are creating a myriad of rituals to continue their relationship with Kian after death, while resuming their lives.

Venkat said, "I have a keychain with Kian's footprints on one side and his handprints on the other (Figure 8.13). Nidhi has a necklace with the same (Figure 8.14). We created an altar at home with pictures of our baby, and we wish him *good morning* and *good night* every day. We organized a fundraiser for Save the Children and will also donate a Cuddle Cot (a cooling unit disguised inside a bassinet which allows parents to keep their baby for two or three days at their bedside during the hospital stay) and donate to other charities for other bereaved parents along with charities that do research on preterm labor in Kian's name."

Nidhi said, "We read to Kian, buy him books, sing to him. We bake cakes on his milestones—the first, scond, third—month on the date of his birth. We take his photo places, talk to him and share things with him. When we go to the beach we write his name in the sand. We dedicated a song to him—*Chasing*

Figure 8.13

Figure 8.14

Figure 8.15

*Cars* by Snow Patrol. I want to make a memorial quilt and take a pottery class and make an urn. We also grow plants, and it feels nice to have some kind of new life at home because we could not bring Kian home. We ordered a memory bear with the clothes he never got to wear. The bear will have his birth weight and height. I heard about this company called Celestis (www.celestis.com) which launches a symbolic portion of cremated remains into near-space and beyond. We might look into that. And we are planning a celebration of life on his six-month birthday making terrariums with our friends and adding rocks with his name on them. We made an online photo memory of Kian to share with our families in India. I paint rocks with his name on them and plan to leave them around town (Figure 8.15). Those things make us feel like we are including him, like he's not completely gone."

Mandy and Sean have found Jewish rituals to be very helpful to honor their son, Jack. Mandy said, "Shiva set us to the rituals from the Jewish playbook. It is a very old playbook, so we did shloshim (the thirtieth day after the burial) and Yahrzeit (anniversary of the death). And Yizkor to light the candle. Each year you light five candles. It's been one of the most anchoring things because I don't feel I have to put my grief on a shelf. Sometimes I get creative ideas like a scrapbook but, at other times, lighting a candle was as much as I could do. "

Sean who, along with Mandy, has always been passionate about the space program, has found solace in thinking about their baby as *the pathfinder*. Mandy said, "This terminology came to us within hours of delivering Jack and saying goodbye to him. We had been moved to a postpartum room and were crying, devastated and frozen. When Sean asked how G-d could do this to us, I responded, 'G-d is benevolent, he is not punishing us. He gave us Jack as a gift. After two back-to-back miscarriages we got to experience nearly nine full months with Jack. He showed us we can go full-term—that is a gift." Upon hearing this, Sean responded, "Jack is a brave pathfinder. He went the farthest and showed us it was possible. We changed so much of our lives while expecting him. He showed me how to be a supportive husband during the pregnancy, he showed us the path."

Mandy said, "The pathfinder in Apollo 8 did not land on the moon. It was a dress rehearsal before a final landing and it allowed the team to practice, and to know that, up to that point, everything is possible. Frank Borman's mission in 1968 was to circle the moon. He's an older guy now, and he's very much a pathfinder, so he gave us this photo inscribed: *To Jack, from one pathfinder to another. Your parents love you very much.* I'm thinking about the astronauts going around the moon and not landing, and feeling they were contributing to the overall mission. For us, Jack was this hero that provided us with the message: *This is how we can get this far, and the Apollo 11 mission came after when they did land on the moon. Without the pathfinder there would be no Neil Armstrong."* In Mandy and Sean's mind, their son paved the way to the safe arrival in his family of his little sister.

Other parents celebrate their babies on October 15th, the National Pregnancy and Infant Loss Remembrance Day (www.nationaldaycalendar.com). Justyna said, "On that day we played the same music we had played when we scattered Matteo's ashes in Hawaii." The whole month of October is dedicated to remembering these kinds of losses.

*    *    *

The different ways grieving parents integrate their baby into their lives after a loss is a reflection of who they are as a couple, as individuals, and of their everlasting love for their child. Simple and private rituals, like lighting a candle, can be powerful in connecting to their child. For others, a grand gesture like sending some of the ashes into space to circle the earth fits their need to place their child within the vastness of the universe. Creating that anchor through rituals allows the parents to rebuild their lives in between those moments. In my experience, this is often a turning point in their healing. As Robert Anderson (1968) expressed: *"Death ends a life, but it does not end a relationship."*

# Memorial Places to Honor Babies

## The Memory Garden At Eternal Home Cemetery[11]

### Description

After suffering pregnancy losses, two San Francisco women, Debbie Findling and Abigail Porth, began to imagine a place where parents like themselves, would-be parents, and others could go to reflect, mourn, and heal in response to their loss.

Both of Jewish faith, they have been working hard for a long time to create a sacred space for people to remember pregnancy and infancy loss. At the time of writing, construction of the garden is still underway in Colma, just south of San Francisco. Even though it is adjacent to the Eternal Home Cemetery, it is not a cemetery and does not contain graves. The brochure describes it as "...a quiet, contemplative place, filled with native California trees, flowers, and plants" and where a "circle of redwood trees surrounds a private space for meditation or ceremonies."

Debbie said, "The landscape architect, who was not Jewish, had a deep understanding of the Jewish rituals and practices that would be helpful. There is a reflective pool, and it's round because he wanted it to mirror the aesthetics of a womb. Around the border are the months of the year that encircle it, both in Hebrew and English with the understanding that somebody would want to stand in the month of their loss, or what would have been their due date (Figure 8.16 and Figure 8.17)."

Figure 8.16

Figure 8.17

## The Vision

The brochure reads, "The Garden will be a sacred place for people to remember losses that are often not acknowledged or talked about--miscarriages, stillbirths, and the death of an infant. The garden fills a void in how Judaism responds to these losses. More families who experience pregnancy and infancy losses are talking openly about them. Many are seeking ways to end the isolation that can accompany such losses, and they are seeking solace and support from within the Jewish community. Traditional Judaism does not allow for a formal burial or funeral for losses from miscarriages and stillbirths or for infants less than thirty days old."

Debbie expressed her need for such a place. "For me, Jews mark time. It is a fabric of most Jewish rituals. Judaism doesn't address stillbirth but I have an emotional need to do something on the anniversary of my stillborn. So I can imagine going to The Memorial Garden on that day to mark my stillborn."

## Use of the Memorial Garden

Even though The Memorial Garden was conceptualized by two Jewish women following their own losses, it will be open to the general population. Debbie talked about how she and Abigail hope it will be used.

"The brilliance of The Memory Garden is that there is no prescribed way of using it. We can imagine how we might use it and how others might use it, but it's really open to whatever you bring to it. It is open to the public, men and women both, to people who are straight and LGBT, to people who have experience in infertility, because we talk a lot about IVF when it's successful but not about IVF when it does not work, someone who has had a miscarriage, or someone who decided to end a pregnancy and wants a place to mark that experience. But once somebody is there, they might have a ceremony led by their clergy and with their community in attendance, or a small ceremony led by them or a friend. They might go there on their own and have a private reflective moment. I imagine someone could go there spontaneously and enjoy the beauty of it.

"Place is very important to honor these losses—even at nine or twelve weeks, it is still a valid loss. So we have no dictation on how it will be used because we want to honor each person's legitimate need and experience to validate how they want to honor that loss.

"No matter when the loss occurred during pregnancy, whether a couple felt ending a pregnancy was the best option for them, or whether a couple was unable to conceive, this garden will serve as a place of reflection and healing and as a place to hold a ceremony if so desired."

## The Little Spirits in Canada

The Little Spirits Garden is a landscaped garden dedicated to the memory of babies lost during pregnancy. It was completed in 2012, and sits within the grounds of the Royal Oak Burial Park, a cemetery in Victoria, British Columbia, Canada.

In an article for BBC Stories, journalist Dougal Shaw describes the garden this way. "Within it are a series of long, concrete plinths, with small grey houses resting on them—these are 'spirit houses,' and each one commemorates a lost child. There are about four hundred houses in the garden, with space for up to three thousand. They have a small womb symbol inscribed inside. Families can customize their houses with their own designs, or leave them bare with just a named inscription."[31]

In the article, a mother who had suffered nine miscarriages expresses how she finds comfort in the garden. "It's really difficult when you have a miscarriage and you don't have a body, because there isn't a physical object. The Little Spirits Garden provides that object for you, which is the house. You can look at this and call it your daughter's spirit house. It feels so good to have a home for her."

Dougal Shaw writes about how the garden was conceived. "The garden was designed by Canadian landscape architects Bill Pechet and Joseph Daly. The inspiration came from Bill Pechet's time in Japan. While there he was struck by a Buddhist tradition known as Jiso—the practice of creating a small, votive statue to mark the death of a child. These are usually placed in temples, which have cemeteries attached to them. During festivals they are adorned with clothing, typically little bonnets woven by parents, and they are all brought out to form a pageant."

Just as parents who have suffered a pregnancy loss recently can have a spirit house, so can women of an older generation, whose pregnancy loss was not acknowledged because of the taboos of the time, and who now have a chance to honor their unborn son or daughter.

# Nine

# Trying Again and Subsequent Pregnancy

*You know the worst case scenario, so you can't get excited. Until you have a healthy, live baby, you can't get ahead of yourselves.*

— Ryan

## Making the Decision

AFTER A LOSS, THE TOPIC OF WHEN to try to get pregnant again often gets raised in counseling in just a few weeks. Because the loss is a trauma, I talk with couples about the importance of having healed significantly in all respects—physically, emotionally, mentally and spiritually—before trying again. I suggest mothers talk to their doctors about their physical healing and readiness to carry a baby and I help them process the emotional side of the decision. For most couples, the discussion of when to try again is accompanied by feelings that were absent in the previous pregnancy.

### Fear of Another loss

All couples I have met with over the years have feared they might lose another baby. Now that they have experienced this deep sorrow, they are terrified they might not be able to handle another loss emotionally.

*Sean.* "I can't put another child into the ground."

*Alex.* "We felt we had a lot of love to give a child, but the future felt very uncertain. We wondered, *Are we doomed? Would we be able to chance getting pregnant again? We knew we wanted more children, but how were we going to get there?*"

## Fear of Not Being Able to Conceive

Couples who had fertility issues were anxious about being able to conceive again and worried that it would take a very long time to get pregnant. Sophie said, "I remember talking about adopting soon after we lost Spencer. My arms felt so empty. Plus we felt we'd been robbed of a baby. Our doctor said she felt comfortable with us trying after about six months. So we went straight to IUI (Intrauterine Insemination). It would have been heartbreaking to keep waiting month after month if we tried naturally."

## Loss of Trust in Medical Providers

Some couples, after a stillbirth, had doubts about the medical care they received toward the end of their pregnancy. Mandy said, "With the second pregnancy there was the realization that we had lost trust in our medical providers. So, we consciously tried to regain that trust by sourcing providers who understood our previous experience and what our family needed. Switching to a new medical provider and hospital was helpful."

## A Divided Loyalty

Couples often feel disloyal toward the baby they lost by trying again, almost as if they are attempting to replace one baby with another. Sophie said, "I remember feeling guilty during the IUI procedure, like I was replacing Spencer, moving on, not grieving her anymore."

In counseling I tell these couples that they do not need to wait until they stop grieving their baby before having a new one. In fact, their grief, which is an expression of love for their baby, can live alongside the love they feel for a new child. Many parents are relieved to know they can feel both grief for the baby they lost while attaching to a new pregnancy.

*Alex & Joel.* As a way to include the baby they had lost into a new family chapter, they would say they wanted to have a *sibling for Hunter.*

*Mandy.* When trying again, she let herself be guided by the *spirit and soul of Jack.* "Having been touched by the soul of our son was one of the most honoring experiences of our lives. So, if we could experience that again, it would be amazing to give Jack a *Little Sib.*"

## Fear vs. Hope

Most couples are faced with the challenge to balance their fear of not succeeding in having a live baby with the hope of finally welcoming a healthy baby into their family.

Aaron said, "We both felt we couldn't not try. Trying felt like the continuation of the grieving process. We felt like we were in limbo and this would be the only way to get out of it." Michelle said, "We wanted to have more experiences and that pushed us forward."

By learning to follow their intuition and talking about their fears and hopes in counseling, most of the couples I meet with eventually make the decision to try to get pregnant again on their own timeline and in a way that fits them best. Some only wait for a few menstrual cycles, while others may wait somewhere between six and twelve months after the loss. Even though parents are still grieving their baby and are afraid of what the future might hold, they eventually know when they are ready to try.

# In Vitro Fertilization (IVF) Experiences

According to the American Society for Reproductive Medicine, 48.5 million couples worldwide experience infertility. In the United States the number is 6.7 million, or one in eight couples.[32] The Centers for Disease Control and Prevention reported that the number of infants born through assisted reproductive technology in 2018, was up 33% from a decade ago.[33] In addition to feeling the emotional impact of a fertility issue, couples often find the financial cost of the treatment to be a major obstacle to becoming parents. Organizations like Resolve have compiled a list of Infertility Financing Programs to assist these couples.[34]

Since many of the couples I have supported over time have used IVF to have a family, I describe below two examples of what many call the "IVF Journey" in order to illustrate what that experience is like.

## Julia & David - an IVF Story

Julia said, "Since a genetic issue was responsible for the loss of our baby, we had a consultation with our doctor who recommended IVF. We had four egg retrievals over a period of twelve months." David added, "Probably the hardest part of the whole thing was waiting while they tested the embryos. It took about two weeks to find out how many of those were viable. The first time we had two viable embryos, and we thought, *Great, these are our two babies.*" Julia explained that after four failed transfers, they now have hope the next one will be successful. "We named our last embryo Ralph but it died in the thaw. We named all the embryos. We gave them silly names that we would not actually give to the baby, just in the hope it would turn into a baby. I now have a very good feeling about the next transfer which will probably be in a couple of months."

David said, "The roller coaster of emotions is incredibly difficult because there are times when you think, *We're almost there, near the finish line, and then further away from it.* We had a bit of optimism and then the door would slam. As a partner, it is very hard to know the right thing to say. If I did say something, it was the wrong thing. If I didn't say anything, that was wrong too. Our entire world revolved around talking about pregnancy. As a partner it would be helpful to divert attention off the topic, but Julia didn't want that—her whole life and schedule revolved around IVF." Julia said, "As women, we cannot escape from IVF because it is a physical, emotional and mental process."

David said, "The only distraction was when we were with friends. I felt like I needed a bit of an escape, and distraction is my best way of coping." Julia found help through an IVF Facebook group. She said, "Finding women who had a situation similar to me was so helpful. I could see that this happens to lots of women—and they go on—it gave me hope. And what I needed from David was not pity—just to be held. And I learned to cope by not having high expectations of success each time."

## Alyssa - an IVF Story

Alyssa said, "I had surgery on my fallopian tubes when I was twenty-two. When we wanted to have kids, we started to try naturally, but it was not happening. I went to a Reproductive Endocrinologist. After reading my medical report the doctor told me my tube was destroyed and suggested we do IVF. We went through the egg retrieval and got twelve embryos. We were very excited. I became pregnant with the first transfer, and we announced my pregnancy at sixteen weeks. But between the eighteenth and the twenty-second week, we found out there was a genetic issue. After a lot of conversations and clinical discussions, we knew we had to end the pregnancy before the twenty-four week mark. Our other embryos have been tested for the genetic defect and are confirmed with 99% accuracy to be normal.

"I learned early on that you get very emotional with IVF—there's a lot of hormones involved and your husband is a great support system, but what you want is to connect with other women who are going through that. The platforms I found were so vast and impersonal, and women were not necessarily uplifting or reassuring. There wasn't a space for positivity. I decided to create a Facebook page, *The IVF Health Journey*, and an Instagram account where the focus was on health and living a positive lifestyle that enhances your chances of conceiving through fertility treatment. I did a lot of research, read a lot of books, met a lot of people along the way, and that is how I had such a positive IVF experience. I educated myself on how to advocate for myself and for other women who were going through it.

"My partner, like a lot of male partners, wants to fix the problem. When he can't fix it he gets frustrated, and then I get frustrated because I know he can't fix it—I just want him to understand. I learned to communicate with my partner, *This is not a problem I need you to fix—only the doctor can fix it—but this is a problem where I need you to listen to me.*

"I wanted to learn how diet and lifestyle changes could affect infertility. I learned that acupuncture can help with the cycle after your transfer, and even during your transfer to help the embryo to stick. I learned that it's better to do low-impact exercise, and that walking was best. I learned about beauty and cleaning products, and how a lot of them have hormone disruptors. I immersed myself in all there was to learn. Doing that helped me feel that I was in more control."

Alyssa also learned to manage her expectations of success. "Setting the expectation, *It's not necessarily going to work, but it doesn't mean it's never going to work was key.* You may hit a lot of hurdles along the way, and some of them may make you feel like it will never happen, but there is always hope that, if you can't have a live baby yourself, you can use a surrogate, adopt, or do embryo adoption."

Alyssa was able to rejoice when other women had successful pregnancies. "A lot of women get very upset when they hear about the success stories, but what they don't realize is that this woman went through what you're going through, and that connecting with that person may help bring you positivity and hope."

## Managing a New Pregnancy

### Anxiety

Many of the couples I had met after they lost a baby returned for support during a subsequent pregnancy. All of them expressed a very high level of anxiety throughout. Unlike the first pregnancy, when they approached each step with joyful anticipation, this time they refrained from getting excited and shied away from family and friends who congratulated them. Very often they refused to have a baby shower and found it very difficult to prepare a nursery. In addition, once they started to feel the baby kick, the mothers felt a mix of excitement and a reluctance to attach to the baby for fear of having another loss.

*Sophie & Ryan.* It was a roller coaster of emotions from the moment Sophie got pregnant. "*Would it happen again?* I remember being very anxious, not feeling I could connect to the pregnancy. I couldn't get excited or get my hopes up. I asked my sister to assemble the nursery. I refused a baby shower—it had been so hard to return everything after Spencer died. With Spencer I took a weekly bump picture. I did not take a single picture this time. That was my way of protecting myself." Ryan said, "I was anxious, too. I didn't talk to anybody at work about the pregnancy until I went on paternity leave."

For couples who experience a second-trimester loss, they are often most stressed during the time leading up to the day they lost their baby.

*Christie.* Needing confirmation she was pregnant for a very long time, she said, "I took a pregnancy test every day until the twentieth week when we lost Archer. It was just for security purposes. We waited until the second trimester to tell our families."

*Rebecca.* "At the beginning we were pretty anxious. I had some spotting and was very scared. Once we got a clear medical scan at the twentieth-week mark, it became a bit more real but I was still reserved. Once something horrible has happened you can never see the world the way you did before."

The couples who had a stillbirth or lost a baby soon after birth experienced high anxiety for the duration of the pregnancy.

*Alex.* "With this pregnancy it felt like we were out on a limb the entire time. I did not sleep much. We lost Hunter during the night, so I was scared. I had to get up and try to breathe."

*Amanda.* "The terror factor was the underlying emotion. Having people tell me not to worry was so out of my reality."

*Mandy.* "For us nothing was a given. I did not want to hear, *Congratulations.* I wanted people to acknowledge that something could come up, and it made me angry when they did not."

A woman I counseled had a termination at the twenty-second week of pregnancy. She was now pregnant again. On the anniversary of the loss of the baby, she posted this message to a support group on Facebook. It captures the sadness over the loss of the previous baby and the attempt to be hopeful about this new one.

*Does anyone feel particularly sentimental in subsequent pregnancies around the same time point as a previous termination? I am pregnant again, and today is the day last time when I started the D&E...I am incredibly thankful that our scan went well a few weeks ago. It's starting to feel real, and my husband and I are slowly allowing ourselves the joy and anticipation of growing our family. But I reflect constantly on the last experience, and allow waves of sadness and remembrance to wash over me. I don't want to forget. I will never forget. You move forward and carry it with you. – Alice*

# Managing the Anxiety

## A different pregnancy & a different baby

While counseling couples, I find it very helpful to give them a few mantras taken from the field of trauma. I tell them. *Say to yourself, This is a different pregnancy, a different baby.* Or, *Say, that was then, this is now.* Because traumatized people get triggered very quickly by experiences similar to those that caused the pain in the past, it is important to help them separate the two experiences by having this sort of inner dialogue. It can also help couples who are waiting for an appointment in the hospital or a doctor's office to get oriented to the room physically and note the differences between the room where they are, in the present time, and the room where they heard bad news in the past.

Sean said, "We would consciously look at the actual appointment room and take in the fact that this was a different day, a different pregnancy and baby, and talk about how things were different—the provider, the room, the art work on the wall—that was super helpful."

## Breaking down time & celebrating each moment

For couples who have lost a baby during pregnancy or infancy, it is very hard to resist projecting themselves into the future. The length of the pregnancy until they can welcome a live baby feels interminable. In counseling I guide these couples to break down time into increments they can tolerate. By staying in the moment, couples are able to appreciate their current reality a bit more easily.

*Alex.* "We would break down time, hour to hour, week to week, ultrasound to ultrasound."

*Rebecca.* "I'd tell myself, *One day at a time*, and *Don't look past the week*. It's so hard to put into practice but it is the only way to do it. This is just a phase, put on blinders, don't think beyond that, like the baby's first Christmas...We would say, *She's still around today.*"

*Christie.* "We just used the doppler and heard the heartbeat—she's okay. It took a lot of talking to myself, *I need to carry this baby, she's going to be fine.*"

*Amandine.* "We learned to celebrate each moment. We have good news today—we want to celebrate that. There may be bad news later, but today all is well. Let's live with what we know, not what we're afraid of."

## Self-Care & Extra Monitoring

Many couples turned to relaxing activities like gardening, yoga, and meditation and also to holistic health treatments like acupuncture. Some distracted themselves from their anxiety by being busy. Some couples took on home improvement projects, such as house remodels.

*Lena.* "I needed to smile, breathe, meditate."

*Rebecca.* "We were very busy during the pregnancy, and found that to be very helpful."

*Alex.* "A major distraction like remodeling was helpful. We needed something to pour ourselves into."

Most couples also sought extra monitoring from their medical providers to manage their anxiety.

*Christie.* "It was so nice when the doctor said, *If you're worried about anything at all, show up at the office.* There were times I was in there just to see the baby's legs kicking. The doctor had a calm voice, he knew all the statistics—it was very reassuring."

*Amanda.* "We needed constant monitoring and saw a Maternal Fetal Medicine doctor for extra support."

*Sophie.* "Our formula was to have extra monitoring. Toward the end I would feel anxious if I had not felt the baby move in two hours. The doctors and nurses told me to go in for my peace of mind whenever I needed to."

*Mandy & Sean.* "We had always been people who did not want to be squeaky wheels, or wanted to put pressure on medical providers," Sean said. "But we realized that we needed to challenge our providers and feel okay with it because that is what we needed." Mandy said, "I learned it was okay to be my own patient advocate. When we had an ultrasound and the technician said, 'It looks normal', I would ask, *How did you come to that line of thinking?*"

## Before & After the Birth

For many couples, each step before the birth—whether it is taking a hospital visit, preparing the basics for the nursery, or packing a hospital bag—feels terrifying, almost as if investing emotionally into these activities might jinx the outcome. People who were not superstitious before the loss are now scared that events out of their control might lead to another loss.

*Mandy & Sean.* Some couples reached out to their community just before a scheduled C-section. Mandy wrote in an email:

> *We want to mark time at this moment, to recognize Little Sib as already part of our family, just like we recognize Jack. We honor the time we have been blessed to experience both Little Sib and Jack in the living world. We recognize that it is often stigmatized to call out the diverse range of outcomes when it comes to pregnancies, but in our case, we can't hide from it—pregnancies can lead to well and unwell babies... We are not getting too ahead of ourselves. Though we are very excited about the potential to meet Little Sib out in the world today, we are instead staying in the moment, being grateful for Little Sib being thirty-seven weeks and four days today. We love her no matter how today goes, and are staying in the moment until the next moment comes.*

*Lena.* Feeling very anxious as the due date came and went, Lena said, "I felt I was ready. I felt she was ready. So, one night at 2 AM I called triage and told them I wanted a C-section, and they agreed. We went in, and it was the same delivery room as before, and we sang the yoga chant—Luis, my cousin, and me. We chanted the whole time and the nurse said it was the most peaceful birth."

*Alex & Joel.* Finding a way to include Hunter in her little sister's birth was important. Alex said, "We talked to Hunter the whole labor, and kept asking her to help the baby to be born alive. We brought in a rock from her beach, and Joel wore a ceramic heart from her memory box. When they pulled her out and she cried, we were overwhelmed with joy—that was the cry we did not hear with Hunter, and that was what we had been waiting for since she passed."

Babies born after a pregnancy or infancy loss are called "rainbow babies"—a symbol of beauty after the storm of the loss and with a challenging dichotomy to navigate. Welcoming a new baby is a very emotional moment, a time when parents are grieving the baby they lost, and feel sadness that this baby is not physically present to welcome his or her little brother or sister. At the same time they are overwhelmed with joy at the sight of their healthy new baby.

Christie said, "Our new baby was kicking her legs, and I got emotional because that was one of the things that was wrong with Archer—he would have been paralyzed. We never saw him move. I remember Wayne and I alone in the room with our new baby, and I thought, I am holding a baby I wanted for so long. I wondered if Archer was helping with that. Our wedding song came on the playlist as we were holding our daughter, and my sister walked in and took a photo."

## Telling the New Baby About Their Older Brother or Sister

Most couples look forward to telling their new child about their older brother and sister as a way to acknowledge their existence and to weave them into the family story.

*Alex & Joel.* Including their first daughter, Hunter, in the announcement of the birth of her sister was important to them. Alex said, "We posted on Instagram, *We welcomed our second daughter.* The nursery is named after both our daughters. When the time is right, we'll tell her about Hunter. I'm excited to tell her about her big sister."

Many parents have shared with me the confusing realization that the new baby would not have existed if the older one had not died.

*Nathalie.* "Now, looking at our daughter, it is strange to think she would not exist if we had not terminated Sam's pregnancy."

*Amanda & Tim.* Talking to their new baby about Jonah feels important. Tim said, "I show him pictures of his brother—he's the oldest but also the second born. The best piece of advice we received was to do what feels right to us, so we want him to know Jonah."

*Lena.* "We tell our new baby about her big sister. She helps me take off my Nayeli necklace, she goes to her altar, and plays with the beads on it. She will play a huge role in honoring her sister."

*Rebecca.* She imagines telling her daughter about her older brother in an age-appropriate way. "I think she'll say, *Oh, I had a brother before me.* I've always been clear that I don't want the weight of John's loss on her, or to even feel she has to be the perfect daughter to make up for the loss. It's not her burden to carry—it's mine, and I accept the emotional weight of it. But it is a part of my life and our family history, so she should know about him."

*Sara.* She loves seeing her daughters play with Lena Bear, the weighted bear given to her by a friend. "I love watching them hug it as though they were hugging their little sister."

*Justyna.* She showed her four-year-old daughter a book of photos she made in honor of Matteo. "I told her, *You are a big sister.* She is old enough now to understand simple relationships. We made a simple family tree and included the baby's photo and that of her grandfather as well. We told her her big brother is with her grandfather. Sometimes, if she thinks I'm sad, she will say, *Are you sad thinking about Matteo? Maybe you can look at his photo to make you feel better.* At the National Pregnancy and Infancy Loss Remembrance Day on October 15th, we played the same music we played when we scattered his ashes in Hawaii."

Katy and Lance have brought their second son to the cemetery where Dominic is buried, and love seeing the brothers reunited at the gravesite (Figure 9.1).

Figure 9.1

# TEN

# Grief Over Time - Lessons Learned

*There is a feeling in my heart that is completely
shattered, and yet it feels a little bit bigger. And leads
to richer relationships.*

— Christine

*The greatest lesson our son taught us was that you wake up
every day and you live it like there is no tomorrow.*

— Amanda

IN ORDER TO SURVIVE TRAUMATIC EXPERIENCES, including the loss of a baby,
people often search for new meaning in their lives and reflect on the positive
and negative impact of the event on themselves. This process of "meaning making" leads people to new assumptions about their world.[35] In *Helping Bereaved
Parents*, Tedeschi and Calhoun suggest a new realization that "events that happen make sense, but not always; that there is disillusionment, yet it is generally
not the disillusionment of despair, but one tempered by hope."[3] Many, although
not all, discover that deep pain can lead to newfound strength in several areas—
a concept called "posttraumatic growth."[36] This is not at all meant to imply that
there is any silver lining in the loss of a baby but rather that parents can emerge
from trauma with improved relationships, with a new sense of strength, and
the resilience to survive most tragedies. Additionally, after trauma, one may
experience an increased appreciation of what matters most. Not everyone will

experience this growth and some will continue feeling the effects of trauma mixed with new strength.

Just as the grief after the loss of a baby is unique to each individual, the areas of posttraumatic growths will also vary from person to person. For example, some parents will carry a higher level of anxiety for a long time after the loss while also feeling a renewed desire to help others struggling with grief. I interviewed couples anywhere from six months to five years after the loss of their baby. With the passing of time they were able to consider the ways in which they had been changed by the experience. Many more parents talked about the growth they had experienced than about the negative effects.

## Lingering Challenges

Several couples reported that the struggle to survive the loss of their baby had made them feel older.

*Amanda.* "We have a lot more grey hair. It took a physical toll. Learning to walk with that and the grief is something I'm still trying to figure out."

*Katherine.* " We recognize that we got much older from the damage caused by losing Neil, both physically and emotionally. The damage is profound and long-lasting. It may not be visible over a couple of weeks, but it is very visible over the years."

Couples often have difficulty trusting friends or family. Or, in particular, medical providers, if they feel more monitoring during their pregnancy might have saved their baby.

*Christie.* "Losing Archer has made me need more time alone and I have difficulty trusting my friends because some of them were critical of our decision to terminate the pregnancy."

*Michelle.* "I am more distrustful of the world, of the medical profession, and of the fairytale idea of pregnancy that is out there. It's also made it very difficult to see people in public who are not appreciating their children or ignore them. They don't realize how fragile life is and how one moment can change everything."

Several women who had had anxiety issues before the loss found their fears had increased.

*Nathalie & Carl.* "I've always had a history of anxiety and it has gotten so much worse," Nathalie said. "It was especially high after our second child was born but it has gotten a little better as she is getting older. That is part of the reason I started therapy again." Carl said, "Of the conflicts we have these days as a couple, the one about Nathalie's anxiety is probably the biggest trigger."

*Julia & David.* When they lost embryos during IVF, they also grieved the loss of the possibility of having either a baby boy or girl. David said, "At first all the embryos were male. I had it in my head that we were going to have a boy. But now all the male embryos are gone, so I won't be able to do the things I did with my dad, like playing soccer. It feels like we've lost four sons. Now we have girl embryos. I'm delighted but I have to adjust in my head to what will now happen."

## Understanding Pain & Supporting Others

The majority of the couples I interviewed had gained a deep understanding of pain and now wanted to extend themselves to others who are struggling with the loss of a baby or face other difficulties.

*Luis & Lena.* "I learned to be kinder," Luis said. "You never know what people are going through. It gave us more compassion." Lena said, "I hope that someday I will be able to help people like us who have lost babies."

*Justyna.* "I had not had much experience with grief, so I learned a lot about it. I feel more sensitive to other people's grief."

*Sara & Jay.* "This has made us stretch more toward others and develop more tolerance for pain and have more compassion. Now I want to advocate for more services for couples who lose a baby."

*Christine.* "When people around me are suffering, I know what that feels like. I feel good about myself when I help people who are going through something—I write them a card, bring them lasagna—I can tolerate their pain and give them a reprieve."

*Mandy.* "I have reached out to strangers who seemed to be upset and asked them, *Are you alright?* I can tune in better to others."

*Aaron.* "I have been more understanding of other people. I realize they may be going through things and I treat them more gently."

# Giving Back in Remembrance of the Baby

Many parents wanted to give other couples hope that they, too, will survive the loss of a baby. Having learned a new sensitivity to people's suffering led many couples to reach out and help in their baby's name.

*Christine & André.* "Our capacity for other people's pain is much bigger and we think of Isla as our inspiration for this."

*Alex & Joel.* "We want to give back in some way and talk to other couples to give them a small hope. It will feel like another way to honor Hunter."

*Sophie & Ryan.* "If I know someone has gone through this, I want to do all I can to support them. Now we understand people better who have had losses and we want to give them confidence they can get through it." In order to explain how she and Ryan felt driven to support people around her, Sophie said, "We have acknowledged that without Spencer we would not have been able to recognize this, as well as now. We are grateful to realize the huge impact she has had on our lives and our friends' lives. Our friends have told us they appreciate their family so much more now because they feel lucky to have healthy children."

# Growing Stronger as a Couple

While soon after the loss of their baby couples often feared their relationship would fall apart, most couples I spoke with actually felt their bond had strengthened significantly.

*Julia & David.* "Obviously, I wish we had not had to go through this but we have certainly grown as a result of this experience and know we can get through anything together," Julia said.

*Nidhi & Venkat.* "I feel very fortunate that we've come to the other side of this tragedy stronger than before." Venkat agreed, "I feel we have grown stronger as a result of this."

*Christie & Wayne.* "We learned to talk to each other more and we feel closer. We go on long drives together so we can talk without distractions," Christie said.

*Sophie & Ryan.* "We're a stronger couple as a result. We just talk about things. We don't avoid things anymore," Sophie said.

*Justyna & Adrien.* "We learned to respect our differences and we did survive this. We made it to the other side even stronger," Justyna said.

*Christine & André.* "We're closer now," Christine said. "André has seen me at my most vulnerable. I was afraid he would get sick of my pain and I asked him, *What if you can't handle it anymore?* That was so hard to say to him. He would say, *I'm not going anywhere.* He's still here and he still loves me. Having been so vulnerable with each other and suffered so much has solidified our bond."

*Mandy & Sean.* "We grew closer together as a couple," Mandy said. "We learned to give each other second chances if the communication did not go well, to take time to give each other the care that was needed, and to be there for each other in a deep way." Sean said, "There is no silver lining to this but it does make you appreciate the importance of supporting each other."

## Surviving Anything

Having survived the worst time in their lives, couples often feel they can overcome future challenges.

*Emily.* "We've pretty much done the worst thing that could have happened to us so we know we're strong enough to get through anything."

*Sean.* "You realize you have the capacity to weather some of the most devastating circumstances and be able to have faith that time will go by and to keep in mind where you want to get to."

*Katy.* "We are much more intentional than before. We can deal with things better than we were able to even while being tired raising two young children."

Some people get to a place where they feel empowered to put themselves out there, particularly in a public way.

*Christine.* "We went to a friend's wedding and I gave a speech. It was amazing. I was able to make everyone feel that strong emotion I have for my friend. Afterwards we danced with joy and abandon. I remember thinking the next day, *We're going to be okay,* and realizing those intense emotions are just not accessible until you have suffered. It gave me hope that those happier moments will come and last longer."

*Lena.* "At my grandmother's celebration of life, a few months after Nayeli died, I spoke. I felt I was commanding space, that all these people were going to be okay, that we were going to be okay. And I thought, *The dead are living through our eyes and so is Nayeli.*"

## Prioritizing

Having experienced such a significant loss in their lives helps many couples realign their priorities, including appreciating their children in a new way.

*Emily.* "I am much more grateful than I ever was for the three kids that we have. I so appreciate Clara as a baby and try to take in every second with her. There is nowhere I'd rather be than with my kids."

*Rebecca.* "Now that I am a mother I am much more detached from the stress of work. It's just work. Losing John gave me perspective that there are more important things."

*Amanda & Tim.* "We feel the power to say, *This is not our priority. I'm going to do this instead,*" Tim said. Amanda added, "We're trying to live as shamelessly as we possibly can. We recently took a three-week sabbatical to be with each other, our new baby and our dog. We got beautifully uninterrupted family time—we got to snuggle the baby and the dog, we talked about Jonah, we were with each other in such a pure way."

## Appreciating Priceless Moments

Most couples learn to be especially thankful for the happy moments they have as a family.

*Aaron.* "I don't take anything for granted anymore. I feel grateful for every moment with Michelle."

*Katy.* "Each life is a miracle. That babies survive is truly amazing. I felt we really wanted our children and I look at being parents very differently, not casually."

*Amandine.* "We learned it is a miracle when things go well but you can't count on it. I used to try to plan the future. Now we know we can't plan or imagine the future, so we try to let go of planning and enjoy the present moment."

*Sophie.* "We appreciate those moments that make you smile. Our mantra now is, *Love, live, laugh and Spencer.*"

## Creating A *New Normal*

As couples moved away from the early stages of grief and started to enjoy parts of their lives once again, they often expressed an ability to successfully incorporate new joys into their sadness. Other parents talked about the search for a *new normal* and the importance of accepting uncertainty in their lives. Some parents reflected on how their perspective on life had changed.

*Michelle.* "I realized that doing all we can doesn't always eliminate the awful things. After what we went through it was like a drape being pulled back, and that caused it to feel very surreal or unfair. But the reality is that so many birth and life experiences exist. And we only have a narrow view of some of them. It has made me less naive and opened me up to see that there is so much more complexity than I can take in."

*Lena.* "I've had to accept that sadness is a part of life and I'm learning to integrate the pain into our life. For me, being outside in nature is grounding. It makes me feel connected to everything."

*Nidhi.* "We were driving to Mendocino and the last stretch was very windy. I felt, *This is our life now, we never know what's around the corner.* One day you see all these beautiful things around you and you're happy—you see all this green and lush landscape flourishing around you. But you don't know what's around the corner. There could be a cliff. We now tell ourselves that every hour and every day is different, that this is our new normal and accepting that is important. Venkat and I now think, *We accept the good things and the difficulties and don't have the expectation that things will be fine, but we also know that we will overcome the difficulties and we will see beauty again."*

*Alex & Joel.* Learning there is often no explanation for painful events in their lives, Alex posted on Facebook:

> *We tried to make sense of the WHY, which we must concede will never be answered. Even though this impossible question will never be answered, we do believe that Hunter teaches us lessons and imparts wisdom on us if we allow ourselves to see it. We see her surrounding us in the beautiful things we witness, as a gentle embrace that she is always here sharing her presence with us. We feel her love when we find just a little bit of peace. We learn from her when we are able to reflect and look forward to the next day with just a little more strength."*

*Christine & André.* Reflecting on the experience of losing Isla and learning more about the mix of emotions involved in grief, Christine said, "We're trying to figure out our new normal and to build our lives around this pain, with this pain. We now know that pain and loss are part of the human experience. There is a big rainbow of emotions that comes with it—anger, despair, sadness, joy. They are all a part of life."

*　　　*　　　*

In the weeks and months following the loss of their baby, couples often find it impossible to imagine that they will ever pull through, let alone gain strength as a result. In counseling I share with them the grief journeys of other parents so they can hold onto that distant hope. As couples tentatively begin shifting their weight from the feelings of sadness to the practicalities of resuming their activities, they start living with opposing feelings. They learn that grief can coexist with new joys, that anxiety can live alongside strength, that suffering can motivate them to help others, and that vulnerability can lead to greater intimacy. And, together as a couple, they have the conviction they can overcome any future obstacles.

Parents often learn to adapt to living in an uncertain world and to shift their focus from planning their future to enjoying the present moment with their loved ones. As they find renewed meaning and reward in their activities, they also frequently redefine their priorities. While venturing into new territory, such as supporting other people who lose a baby, these couples often do so in remembrance of their baby. Using their child as an inspiration to help other grieving parents provides a positive and enduring attachment to their baby going forward and does not constitute denial of the loss. Incorporating experiences of personal growth into one's grief is an essential part of the healing process. Pain and joy, emotional scars and determination, vulnerability and strength—somehow—become the companions of many bereaved parents.

It is important to note that substantive growth in the aftermath of the loss of a baby does not occur in all grieving parents. It seems to have been the case with the couples I interviewed and the majority of other parents I have supported over the years, but I am very aware that some people may remain traumatized for a very long time, especially those who do not have access to grief counseling or treatments such as EMDR or acupuncture or who do not have a supportive social network.

As I mentioned earlier, the couples I interviewed were fairly homogeneous—upper and middle class, educated, and primarily caucasian. I strongly recommend that more grief counseling services be made available for minority, low-income populations, which also means recruiting and training counselors of varied backgrounds. As a society, the barriers tied to asking for help when suffering a loss need to be removed.

For example, speaking for African American women who suffer twice as many pregnancy and infancy losses than white women, neonatologist Terri Major-Kincade, MD, MPH, points to barriers to accessing bereavement support in the African American community.[38] She recommends helping bereaved women of color find racially diverse support groups to promote a sense of belonging, as well as putting them in touch with other African American women who have also experienced the loss of a baby. With this in mind, I acknowledge that my words and those of the couples I interviewed may not represent the experience of all groups. I would support engaging in conversations about this topic with a more racially and culturally varied group of grief counselors and bereaved parents.

# Conclusion

WHETHER YOU, MY READER, are a grieving parent or a friend, or a family member of someone who has lost a baby, my hope is for you to find some solace and guidance in the reflections of the couples I interviewed. These parents were motivated by the desire to help other couples who lose babies and to give them hope they too could survive this tragedy. It has been an honor for me to share these stories of lasting love.

Here are some takeaways to remember during difficult times:

- Grief is unique to each individual and couple. Different grieving styles need to be respected.

- Grief does not occur in neat stages and is not concluded in a set period of time.

- Sharing stories of the death and memories of the pregnancy, or of the baby's short life, provides new connections between parent and child.

- In the initial phase of the grief, family and friends can best support a grieving parent by just listening when they need to talk and providing practical help the rest of the time.

- Most parents appreciate family and friends using the baby's name and remembering dates such as the birthday or anniversary of the death.

- Grief evolves over time and it is important to continue to give voice to one's emotions. Ultimately, sadness will mix with new joys, and vulnerability with new strengths, as parents create a *new normal.*

- Experiences of personal growth mix with grief and do not represent denial of grief. What seems most important is for parents to form a new bond with their baby after death.

For the couples I spoke with, the act of being interviewed and having to put one's grief into words helped them continue to process their loss. For many it gave them a new sense of *healing* and *empowerment*. I imagine these parents will continue to look at their grief in different ways in the years to come and I wonder if a periodic check-in with a grief counselor, privately or in a facilitated support group, or participation in a grief retreat with other couples, might be helpful.

While moving forward with their lives, parents often find comfort in creating a legacy in remembrance of their baby or by the practice of living their lives "through their baby's lens." They find it helpful to think or say, *Jack would want us to do…* or *We're doing this so Jack would be proud of us.* Not only does this transform the loss into meaningful contributions, but it also helps bring the memory of the baby into the parents' ongoing lives.

As Thomas Attig said,

Consciously remembering those who have died is the key that opens our hearts, that allows us to love them in new ways. As we remember what we love about those who have died, we welcome them back into our lives even though we are apart. We begin to learn how to love them in new ways. In memory we can cherish them. We can carry them with us into the future.[39]

# Acknowledgments

ABOVE ALL, I AM deeply indebted to the couples I interviewed. They so generously shared the stories of the most painful time in their lives in order to help other parents facing a similar loss in the future. It truly was a privilege to be allowed to accompany you in your grief journey and to learn from you how one can survive such a loss. Thank you for sharing your love for your baby as well as your deepest pain and learned wisdom. I know that your baby's story and your words of guidance and support will have a significant impact on many people's lives. Many thanks also go to the other eighty bereaved couples I have supported over the years. The way you navigated your grief over time has inspired me and taught me more than you will ever know.

My profound appreciation goes to Vera Russell, BSW, MPH, for teaching me the theoretical underpinnings of Kitchen Table Counseling and for guiding me in the practice of this work repeatedly over the years. Your generous teachings and support have led to a friendship I value deeply.

Similar thanks go to Summer Segal, PhD, for the many helpful discussions about pregnancy and infancy loss we have had over the years. Your depth of knowledge, compassion and wisdom have helped improve the quality of my work immensely, and I treasure the friendship which has resulted.

My special thanks go to Kathy Hull, PsyD, founder of George Mark Children's House in San Leandro, CA, for writing the foreword to this book. Your deep professional knowledge of this work and your compassion add to my words in a very meaningful way.

This book would not have come into existence as smoothly as it did without the expert assistance of my editor, Janine Noël. You understood my vision and used your wise editing and knowledge of the craft of writing to make my words as clear as possible. I deeply appreciated your reassurance that my writing as a non-native English speaker conveyed my meaning sufficiently well. Thank you from the bottom of my heart for your collaboration and encouragement as well as for your kindness and laser-like focus and edits.

What a joy and immense relief to have benefited from the technical expertise of my son, Nicky Evers. You have taught me all I know about using the computer. With endless patience, skill, incomparable love, and warmth, you have taught me all I know about using the computer, and helped make this book possible. I am in awe of the man you have become and so thankful for your help with this book.

To my publisher at Kat Biggie Press, Alexa Bigwarfe, and her talented team, I owe a huge debt of gratitude. I knew from the beginning that I was in very competent hands, and so appreciated your patience, enthusiasm and skill. My deepest thanks to Michelle Fairbanks of Fresh Design for the book cover, and to Alexa's team - Nancy Cavillones, Raewyn Sangari, and Sarah O'Dell - for the preparation for publishing and marketing of the book.

Many thanks to Adam Jacobs of Adam Jacobs Photography for taking a lovely headshot for this book. I am so appreciative of your talent and kindness.

My mother, Marie-Josèphe Vermont, and my grandmother, Marguerite Bailleul, taught me invaluable lessons in serving others, especially the dying and their loved ones. Up until her death at age 96, my grandmother sat at the bedside of "old people" as they lay dying. By following in their footsteps and supporting those in grief, I hope to honor them and express my love for them.

I am eternally grateful to Howard Treisman for his belief, years ago, in the value of my work and for helping me find the confidence I needed to reach a wider audience. Your support, love and comments have, in part, led to the writing of this book, and your encouragement has inspired my mission to accompany future grieving parents.

I am blessed with the friendship of so many wonderful people. Thank you so much for understanding my passion for this topic and for believing I could actually accomplish this task. I will always be grateful for your love, laughter, and support when I truly needed it. Among many others, I especially want to acknowledge Adam and Lucy Kernan-Schloss, April Matthews, Bruno and Jan Caire, Dale and Bruce Wheeler, Dan Rosen, Elia Makar, Elliot Evers, Greta Treisman, Joan Fries, John Leupold, Lauren Matthews, Monique Urmès, Nancy

Deutsch, Naomi Porat, and Paola Orozco Gallegos. To anyone unnamed, my apologies and gratitude to each of you.

Thanks and "bisous" to my grandchildren, Samory, Sassondella and Gañesiri, for giving me a new understanding of love and joy. Your hugs and unconditional love feed me in very important ways.

Finally, my most profound gratitude to my children, Cécile, Vanessa and Nicky. Your love and unwavering belief in my ability to write this book, and deep understanding of its intended goal, have touched and uplifted me more than I can express. You have added a much greater depth to my life than I could ever have imagined possible, and I keep finding new reasons to love you as we all grow together.

# Endnotes

1. Vera Russell, BSW, MPH, Bereavement Counsellor, Sydney Children's Hospital, Sydney, Australia.

2. Association for Death Education and Counseling. www.adec.org.

3. Tedeschi, R. G. & Calhoun, L. G. Helping Bereaved Parents. New York, NY: Brunner-Routledge, 2004.

4. Centers for Disease Control and Prevention. What is stillbirth? National Center on Birth Defects and Developmental Disabilities, August 29, 2019. cdc.gov/ncbdd/stillbirth/facts/html.

5. MacDorman, M.F. & Gregory, E. D., Fetal and perinatal mortality: United States, 2013. National vital statistics reports: from the Centers for Disease Control and Prevention, National Center for Health Statistics, National Vital Statistics System. 2015; 64(8): 1-24.

6. Centers for Disease Control and Prevention. Division of Reproductive Health, National Center for Chronic Disease Prevention and Health Promotion, 3/27/19. cdc.gov/reproductivehealth/maternalinfanthealth/infantmortality.html.

7. Now I Lay Me Down to Sleep. www.nowilaymedowntosleep.org.

8. Institute for the Advancement of Medicine Neonatal Donor Program. www.iiam.org/neonatal-donation/

9. George Mark Children's House. San Leandro, CA: www.georgemark.org

10. Gibran, Kahlil. The Prophet: Alfred, A. Knopf. New York, NY, 1928.

11. The Memory Garden. Colma, CA. www.thememorygarden.org

12. Neimeyer, R. A. Lessons of Loss: A guide to coping. New York, NY: McGraw-Hill, 1998.

13. Parkes, C. M. Psycho-social transitions: A field for study. Social Science and Medicine, 5, pp. 101-115. 1970.

14. Corr, C. A. Revisiting the concept of disenfranchised grief. In Doka, K. J. (Ed.), Disenfranchised grief: New directions, challenges, and strategies for practice (pp. 39-60). Champain, Il.: Research Press, 2002.

15. Wallerstedt, C. & Higgins, P. Facilitating perinatal grieving between the mother and the father. Journal of Obstetrics and Gynecology and Neonatal Nursing, 25 (5), pp. 389-394. 1996.

16. The Milk Bank. www.themilkbank.org.

17. The Dougy Center, Portland, OR. www.dougy.org.

18. Lands, Amie. Navigating the Unknown: An immediate guide when experiencing the loss of your baby. Columbia, SC: Kat Biggie Press, 2017.

19. Juanita de Sanz, MS, LMFT. www.juanitadesanz.com

20. The Compassionate Friends. www.compassionatefriends.org.

21. HAND, Helping After Neonatal Death. www.handonline.org.

22. Klass, D. The deceased child in the psychic and social worlds of bereaved parents during the resolution of grief, in D. Klass, R. Silverman & Nickman (Eds.) Continuing Bonds: New Understandings of Grief. Washington, DC: Taylor & Francis, 1996.

23. Stroebe, M., & Schut, H. The dual process model of coping with bereavement: Rationale and description. Death Studies, 23, pp. 197-224. 1999.

24. Martin, T. L., & Doka, K. J. Men Don't Cry, Women Do: Transcending gender stereotypes of grief. Philadelphia, PA: Brunner/Mazel, 2000.

25. Schwab, R. Effects of a child's death on the marital relationship: a preliminary study. Death Studies, 16 (2), pp. 141-154. 1992.

26. Gilbert, K. R. 'We've had the same loss, why don't we have the same grief?' Loss and differential grief in families. Death Studies, 20 (3), pp. 269-283. 1996.

27. Klass, D., & Silverman, P. R., & Nickman, S. L. (Eds.). Continuing Bonds: New Understandings of Grief. Washington, DC: Taylor & Francis, 1996.

28. Field, N. P. (Ed.). Continuing bonds in adaptation to bereavement: I. Theoretical and empirical foundations; II. Clinical and cultural considerations. Death studies, 30 (8 & 9). 2006.

29. Attig, T. Holiday sorrows and precious gifts. 2013. http://www.griefsheart.com/holidaysorrows.php.

30. Callier, V. Baby's cells can manipulate mom's body for decades. September 2, 2015. www.smithsonianmag.com.

31. Shaw, D. The garden helping to heal the pain of pregnancy loss. BBC Stories. June 19, 2019. www.bbc.co.uk.

32. American Society for Reproductive Medicine. The Society of Reproductive Surgeons - quick facts about infertility between 1987 and 2015. www.asrm.org.

33. Centers for Disease Control and Prevention. ART success rates. cdc.gov. art/artdata/index.html.

34. Resolve. Infertility Financing Programs. Resolve.org/what-are-my-options/making-infeertility-affordable/infeertility-financing-programs/

35. Park, C. L. Implications of posttraumatic growth for individuals. In R. G. Tedeschi, C. L. Park, & L. G. Calhoun (Eds.). Posttraumatic Growth. Mahwah, NJ: Lawrence Erlbaum. 1998.

36. Janoff-Bulman, R. Shattered Assumptions: Toward a new psychology of trauma. New York, NY: Free Press, 1992.

37. Tedeschi, R. G. & Calhoun, L. G.

38. Challenging the Black Superwoman Mentality in the Black Community after Pregnancy and Infant Loss. Webinar hosting Dr. Terri Major-Kincade, June 24, 2020. Return to Zero: H.O.P.E. www.rtzhope.org.

39. Attig, T. The Heart of Grief: Death and the search for lasting love. New York, NY: Oxford University Press, 2000.

# Bibliography and Resources

## Terminal Diagnosis During Pregnancy

Davis, Deborah, L., PhD. Loving and Letting Go. Centering Corporation, 1993

Fertel, Patricia. Difficult Decisions. Centering corporation, 1988.

Kuebelbeck, Amy. Waiting with Gabriel. Loyola Press, 2003.

Kuebelbeck, Amy & Davis, Deborah, L., PhD. A Gift of Time. Baltimore, MD: Johns Hopkins University Press, 2011.

## Grief Support

Clark-Coates, Zoe. Saying Goodbye: A Personal Story of Baby Loss and 90 Days of Support to Walk you Through Grief. Colorado Springs, CO: David. C. Cook, 2017.

D'Arcy, Paula. When People Grieve: Guidance for Grievers and the Friends who Care. New York, Crossroads, 2013.

Davis, Deborah, L., PhD. Empty Cradle, Broken Heart: Surviving the Death of your Baby. Golden, CO: Fulcrum, 1991.

Davis, Deborah, L., PhD. Stillbirth, Yet Still Born. Golden, CO: Fulcrum, 2014.

Johnson, S. M. Dr. & Johnson, Joy. This Little While. Centering Corporation, 2000.

Keating, Catherine, N. There Was Supposed to be A Baby: A Guide to Healing after Pregnancy Loss. Seattle, WA: Hummingbird Press, 2012.

Lothrop, Hannah. Losing Your Baby in Pregnancy or the First Year. Fisher Books, 1997.

Lands, Amie. Navigating the Unknown: An Immediate Guide when Experiencing the Loss of your Baby. Columbia, SC: Kat Biggie Press, 2017.

Lands, Amie. Our Only Time: Stories of Pregnancy/Infant Loss with Strategies for Health Professionals. Columbia, SC: Kat Biggie Press, 2017.

McCracken, Anne & Semel, Mary. A Broken Heart Still Beats: After your Child Dies. Hazelden Publishing, 2000.

McCracken, Elizabeth. An Exact Replica of a Figment of my Imagination. Back Bay Books, 2008.

Raeburn, Daniel. Vessels: A Love Story. New York, NY: Norton, 2016.

Schwiebert, Pat, RN & Kirk, Paul, MD. When Hello Means Goodbye. Portland, OR: Grief Watch, 2015.

Wolfelt, Alan, D., PhD & Maloney, Raelynn, PhD. Healing Your Grieving Heart After Stillbirth. Fort Collins, CO: Companion Press, 2013.

## Books for Mothers

Bigwarfe, Alexa. Sunshine After the Storm: A Survival Guide for the Grieving Mother. Columbia, SC: Kat Biggie Press, 2013.

Long, Emily. Love Letters from Loss Mom to Loss Mom. Burlington, VT: Firefly Grace, 2016.

## Books for Fathers

Farley, K & DiCola, D. Grieving Dads: To the Brink and Back. Grieving Dads, 2012

Long, Emily. From Father to Father: Letters from Loss Dad to Loss Dad. Burlington, VT: Firefly Grace, 2016.

Nelson, Tim. A Guide for Fathers: When a Baby Dies. Tim Nelson, 2004.

## Books for Couples

Ilse, Cherokee & Nelson, Tim. Couple Communication After a Baby Dies. Maple Plain, MN: Wintergreen Press, 2008.

Lister, Marcie & Lovell. Healing Together. Centering Corporation, 2004.

## Books for Children

Dougy Center Staff. After a death: An activity Book for Children. Portland, OR: Dougy Center. www.dougy.org.

Dougy Center Staff. Helping Children Cope with Death. Portland, OR: Dougy Center,1997, 2004. www.dougy.org.

Dougy Center Staff. Thirty-Five Ways to Help a Grieving Child. Dougy Center, 1999. www.dougy.org.

Lands, Amie. Perfectly Imperfect Family. Thirty-Three Press, 2019.

Mood, Pat & Whittaker, Lesley. Finding a Way Through When Someone Close Has Died. London, UK: Jessica Kingsley Publishers, 2001.

## Books for Grandparents

Schwiebert, Pat, RN. A Grandparent's Sorrow. Portland, OR: Grief Watch, 2012.

Wolfelt, Alan. Healing a Grandparent's Grieving Heart: 100 Practical Ideas After Your Grandchild Dies. Companion Press, 2014.

## Pregnancy After Loss

Cox, Franchesca. Celebrating Pregnancy Again: Restoring the Lost Joys of Pregnancy After the Loss of a Child. CreateSpace Publishing, 2013.

Lanham, Carol, C. Pregnancy After a Loss. Berkeley, 1999.

Long, Emily & Henke, Lindsey. Pregnancy After Loss Support: Love Letters to Moms Pregnant After Loss. Firefly Grace Publishing, 2020.

Sussman, John, R. Trying Again: A Guide to Pregnancy After Miscarriage, Stillbirth and Infant Loss. Lanham, MD: Taylor Trade Publishing, 2000.

## Preparing For IVF

Chavarro, Jorge & Willett, Walter & Skerrett, Patrick. The Fertility Diet. New York, NY: McGraw-Hill, 2007.

Fett, Rebecca. It Starts With The Egg. Franklin Fox Publishing, 2014.

Nichols, Lily. Real Food For Pregnancy: The Science and Wisdom. Lily Nichols, 2018.

## Remembrance Online Resources

Celestis. Memorial Spaceflight. www.celestis.com

Comfort Cub (Weighted Teddy Bear). www.thecomfortcub.com.

Molly Bears (Weighted Teddy Bears). www.mollybears.com.

National Star Registry (Naming a Star After Someone). www.starregistry.com.

## Grief Support Online Resources

The Compassionate Friends. www.compassionatefriends.org

Ending a Wanted Pregnancy. www.endingawantedpregnancy.com.

Faces of Loss, Faces of Hope (Putting a Face on Miscarriage, Stillbirth and infant loss). www.facesofloss.com.

Glow In The Woods: For Babyloss Mothers and Fathers. www.glowinthewoods.com

Helping After Neonatal Death. www.handonline.org.

Healing Embrace: Helping Everyone after Loss. www.healingembrace.org.

Instagram IVF: @healthyivf

IVF Facebook: IVF Health Journey

The Mariposa Trust (Support for Pregnancy and Infancy Loss). www.mariposa.org.

The MISS Foundation (Counseling, Advocacy, Research, Education for Families Experiencing the Death of a Child). www.missfoundation.org.

Pregnancy After Loss. www.pregnancyafterloss.com.

Resolve - Family Building Options. The National Infertility Association. www.resolve.org/family-building-options.

Return to Zero: H.O.P.E. Pregnancy and Infant Loss Support. www.rtzhope.org.

The Ruthie Lou Foundation (Resources, Support and Hope for Families whose Baby has Died Before, During or Shortly After Birth). www.ruthielou-foundaiton.org.

Star Legacy Foundation (Stillbirth, Education, Research and Awareness). www.starlegacyfoundation.org.

Still Mothers (Living Childless After Loss). www.stillmothers.com.

Still Standing Magazine (Child loss and infertility). www.stillstandingmaga-zine.com.

Sunshine After The Storm: A Survival Guide For The Grieving. https://sun-shineafterthestorm.org

Through The Heart (Pregnancy Loss and Infertility). www.throughtheheart.org.

Twinless Twins (Support for both Twinless Twins and Parents). www.twinless-twin.org.

Twinslist (Support for those who have Experienced the Loss of a Twin, Triplet, or Higher Order Multiple Child). www.twinslist.org.

Unspoken Grief (Community Building and Support to Individuals and Families who Experience Miscarriage, Stillbirth and Infancy Loss). www.unspokengrief.com.

# About the Author

As a clinical psychologist, Pascale Vermont, PhD, has held many positions. She was a family therapist in her early career until her interest turned to the field of death and dying. She became a palliative care counselor, supporting the dying and their families, for a few years before training to work as a grief counselor, first to adults who lost a loved one, and then to parents whose babies died during pregnancy and infancy - work she is continuing up to the present and which she is passionate about.

Pascale has always been interested in crisis and trauma counseling and in disaster mental health. She has trained prospective paramedics in handling sudden death in the field , and staff of a pediatric palliative care home in burnout prevention and self-care. As a volunteer for the American Red Cross for 8 years, she has been deployed to Louisiana, Texas, Arkansas, and Alabama to provide grief counseling to people affected by tornadoes, floods and hurricanes. In addition, Pascale joined an international humanitarian organization ten years ago and has worked in places like Bangladesh, Haiti, Kenya, the Philippines and South Sudan as a trauma and grief counselor and as an instructor of stress management and self-care to staff working in those countries under challenging conditions.

# Parents' Voices After Publication

"Sometimes I don't know how we survived losing our son, and in reading this book I was reminded that we survived by taking many, many small steps. Pascale brings together the words of different families who have experienced the death of a child, and shows both commonalities in their grief and also unique choices each family has made as they integrated their heartbreak into their lives. I would recommend this book to any grieving parent as a light to have in a dark time."

— **Michelle,**
bereaved parent

"I wish someone had given me this book when we lost our son at 24 weeks almost three years ago. The accounts included are raw and heartfelt, accurately capturing those shattering feelings of bereavement while still providing hope for those reading them. I nodded along to all the chapters as I read others' stories intermingled with my own, and this made me feel less alone in my grief."

— **Julia and David,**
bereaved parents

"I received so much healing through the process of therapy and the insights Pascale has shared in this book. I highly recommend this book to parents, extended family, and loved ones who are looking for guidance during this darkest of times."

— **Rebecca,**
mother of John

"I was reminded that as permanent as grief may feel, we can be in community through the written word in hearing about how other families have navigated their own losses. I am eternally grateful for the wisdom and counsel that Pascale provided us, which is now encapsulated in this important book."

— **Sara and Jay,** bereaved parents

"I appreciate Pascale's ability to showcase the spectrum of shock, despair, acceptance and eventually hope, all of which can clash with each other. We did not know how to navigate our daughter's death, and something like this would have been helpful during the times we were not with Pascale. Thank you for creating this guide, Pascale, and for sharing our stories."

— **Christine and André**

"This book brings a deeper understanding through the aftermath of a baby's death. It is a guiding light of support for providers, community, families and, especially, parents. You are not alone."

— **Luis and Lena Soria**

"This beautifully written book helps navigate what to say or not to say through heartfelt and real stories from parents who live through the loss of their baby everyday. If we had not been able to have first-hand experience with Pascale, this book would have been what we would have reached for."

— **Christie and Wayne,** Archer's parents

"Reading this book, even three years later, I experienced a sense of validation, normalization, and connection with the mothers Pascale writes about. I know Pascale's messages would have been helpful for my family to better support me and my husband. She covers many facets and stages of grief, not just surviving it, but stories about moving forward with life again."

— **Nathalie**

"*Surviving the Unimaginable* not only shares raw, honest stories of couples who have lost their baby, but also includes practical steps that parents can take throughout the grieving process to help them cope and find strength during uncertain times. Pascale does a wonderful job of gently guiding parents through what to expect when you lose a baby. I wish a book like this existed when we lost our daughter."

— **Sophie,**
mother of Spencer and two rainbow babies

"This book is crucial for that first year following the loss, especially if a couple starts to think about trying again for a subsequent pregnancy. As a bereaved mother, I found Pascale's words to be relatable and comforting. She holds your hand through the pages as you walk through the unimaginable."

— **Alyssa,**
a bereaved mother

"Pascale offers a precious resource to every person - parents, family, friends, caregivers - facing perinatal death. After my baby died, learning more about grief helped me. This book will be my companion to educate people around me about this special type of grief."

— **Amandine,**
mother of Tino

"After the loss of our first daughter, Pascale's in-person grief counseling was always deeply empathetic and focused on guiding us through the many questions and unfamiliar emotions and challenges that we faced. This book only extends her compassionate reach to educate all people involved in the grief and recovery process."

— **Hunter's**
parents

"It is still impossible to put into words all the feelings that came up for us, and still do, regarding the sudden and unexpected loss of our son Jack. We miss him dearly. Pascale's care in providing us validation gave us hope that there was a healing process to address the overwhelming devastation we experienced in our crisis - and that process need not require us to dismiss, forget or ever let go of our beloved, late son Jack."

— **Mandy and Sean,**
parents of Jack

"As a bereaved Dad, I wish I had read this book earlier to help me grieve better by reading others' experiences of perinatal loss. I found myself immersed in every section. I cannot recommend this book enough - it is an amazing guide for you or anyone you know facing a future without their baby."

— **Venkat,**
father of Kian

"When we lost our daughter it felt important to read about others who survived the horrible pain we were living through, and to take solace and advice from their experiences. Pascale's generosity of spirit as someone who leads people through these dark moments comes through in her words and guidance. I read many books after our daughter died, and this is one I will highly recommend to anyone in our situation."

— **Emily and Gerald,**
bereaved parents

*"Surviving the Unimaginable* was both touching and comforting. I didn't feel alone anymore in this tragedy. All the details provided by parents going through the same process helped me to connect with them instantly."

— **Justyna,**
little angel Matteo's mother, Switzerland

"*Surviving the Unimaginable* helps parents understand that they are not alone, that their child's short life will have deep meaning, and that despite the immense pain, they can learn to walk through the world again. To those who find themselves in the difficult position of saying goodbye to a child much too soon, this book will offer practical wisdom, advice from those who have taken this journey, and most importantly, hope."

— **Amanda,**
Jonah's mom

"*Surviving the Unimaginable* is the book I wish I had when we survived such a loss recently. I trust that it will bring solace to many others, as it has for me."

— **Alice Zheng, MD,**
healthcare consultant, and bereaved parent